*Dedicated to the men,
women and children who
braved the elements and
risked their lives to
live the American dream.
Their hopes live on, both in
their descendants and the
country they helped create.*

MY FOLKS AND THE LAND OF OPPORTUNITY

A Treasury of Immigration Stories
Shared by the Readers of
Capper's and Grit

CAPPER
PRESS

Editor
Samantha Adams

Assistant to the Editor
Patricia Patterson Thompson

Production and Illustrations
Bruce Bealmear

Copyright © 1995
by Capper Press
Printed in the United States of America

ISBN: 0-941678-47-4

FOREWORD

Imagine for a moment that you are an Irish citizen eking out an existence during the horrible potato famine of 1845-46. Perhaps it is the turn of the century, and you are the second son of a Norwegian family, destined to work in a menial job for low wages because your older brother will inherit the family farm. Or maybe a letter from a prosperous cousin in the New World has struck you with wanderlust. For these reasons and many more, you might say good-bye to family and friends, sell your possessions or borrow money for your ship fare, and set sail for America, the Land of Opportunity.

Those who immigrated to America during the 19th and early 20th century were not the first to try their luck in the New World; nor were they all European. But the masses who fled Europe—especially from 1830 to 1930—sailing primarily from the port of Liverpool, England, represented the last great influx of immigrants to America. The potpourri of cultures and traditions they brought with them contributed to the creation of the world's greatest melting pot.

Plagued by famine and war, enticed by the promise of riches and plenty, immigrants came in droves to turn-of-the-century America. *My Folks and the Land of Opportunity* chronicles the trials and tribulations these newcomers—as well as their predecessors and those who have migrated since—faced during their journeys to the promised land, as well as the hardships and triumphs they experienced as they made new lives for themselves and their families. Some immigrants struggled with language barriers or fell victim to fast-talking con men, and many pined for their villages and families back home. But the majority overcame the obstacles, dug their heels in and thanked God for their chance to start anew in the land of plenty.

My Folks And The Land Of Opportunity is the seventh volume in the *My Folks* series that includes: *My Folks Came In A Covered Wagon, My Folks Claimed The Plains, My Folks And The One-Room Schoolhouse, My Folks' Depression Days, My Folks And The Civil War* and *My Folks And World War II.* The opinions expressed are those of the contributors. We make no claim to complete historical accuracy; minor spelling, grammar and punctuation corrections were made to facilitate reading while maintaining the authors' spirit and style.

America would not be the country we know today if not for the brave souls who risked everything to sail to a new world and a new life. For their courageousness and contributions to their adopted homeland, we will be forever indebted.

Samantha Adams
Editor

CONTENTS

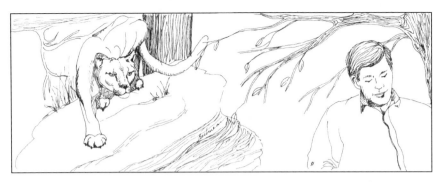

Chapter One: Origins in the British Isles

Ancestor Was a Stowaway

My husband's aunt lived in Washington D.C. for several years. Through researching some of the early Stuart settlers in this country, she found the history of the first Stuart immigrant to the United States. His first name wasn't mentioned in any of the findings. We know he was from Scotland, and we think the circumstances of his entry into the United States played a big part in keeping his name unknown to our family in Tennessee as well as to family members in other states. I'm sure there are other Stuarts who have researched their heritage more extensively than we have, because it has been several years since my husband's aunt first started tracing ours.

Last year in August, the Stuarts held their first family reunion in Cleveland, Tennessee. We met cousins and many Stuarts we had never heard of, and what a day we had. I think we did more talking than eating. This reunion has sparked the curiosity of many Stuarts in Tennessee, Illinois, Indiana and Florida just to mention a few, who plan to continue the search for more Stuarts living anywhere in the United States. My husband and I enjoyed the day tremendously; however, after meeting all of them and trying to remember names and places of residences, we never heard one single Stuart tell of the first Stuart to enter this country.

If my memory serves me correctly, and I think it does—I don't think I could ever forget something as exciting and mysterious as this story told to me by my husband's grandmother—this is supposed to be kept secret, but as we all know nothing can be kept secret forever. The first Stuart came to America as a stowaway on a ship from his hometown because he had fought and killed a man in a boxing match, which carried a prison sentence or possible execution in those days. We know the Stuarts have a reputation for standing their ground with anyone who crosses their path—intentionally or unintentionally.

My husband's grandfather was a foreman in several lumber camps in the late 1800s and the early 1900s, from Tennessee to the hills and mountains of Chico, California. He always took Grandmother Stuart with him and built a cabin near his camp until it was time to move to another area of the vast forest of trees to be cut and milled into the fine woods used in that era.

I remember an exciting story Grandmother told me one night about their life in the hills of Chico, California. She told of preparing Grandfather Stuart's dinner bucket. She made biscuits spread with jelly or meat of some kind. She also made fried fruit pies, all of which were put in a pail for his noontime meal. Sometimes he would work late and walk home long after dark, with only a candle in a bucket for a light to help guide him along the path to the cabin. It was about a mile from the lumber camp. While walking home from work, he often heard footsteps close by. He thought it was only a dog. When the animal would get within a few feet of him, he would shake his dinner bucket at the animal to scare it away for a few minutes. Soon the animal was near him again. This was something he experienced often on his way home from work. One night the animal followed him most of the way home, almost to the cabin door. Grandmother saw the animal and realized the danger he was in. She screamed to him that a mountain lion was at his side. She quickly opened the door and he dashed to safety.

The most mysterious story she told me was of their life in the many lumber camps across this country. Grandfather Stuart was a fearless, quiet, respectable man, but a man could be pushed just so far: beyond that point his opponent had the devil to contend with. Although he was a relatively small man, he could whip, "with only his fist" any man in any of the lumber camps for miles around. The men of those lumber camps soon found this to be true as they often held fist-fighting matches between the different lumber camps. Along the mountain path that Grandfather Stuart walked to the lumber camp lived an old Indian man who proudly displayed a number of white women's scalps of long black, blonde, brunette and red hair. With no accusations made, the old Indian man disappeared one day and was never seen again.

Ruth Stuart
Soddy Daisy, Tennessee

Spinning Wheel Symbolized Pioneer Spirit

Grandfather Grant was a merchant in Shieldaig, Ross Shire, Scotland. His business occupied the lower floor of a stone building that still stands and is still occupied by a store. His family, which included five girls and two boys, resided in the upper story of this building.

Grandfather also had a partnership in three merchant boats that plied the coast of Scotland, furnishing merchandise to small communities. His favorite ship was called *The Agnes,* and it was during a voyage on this ship that Grandfather became ill. Mother was a child at the time but remembered going with the family to meet her father as the boat entered the harbor. It was his custom to be on deck to wave a greeting to the family. When he did not appear her mother said, "Children, your father is ill." Grandfather was carried to his home and lived only a short time.

In her youth, Grandmother had been educated in both culture and homemaking, having attended a school where domestics and etiquette predominated. There is in our family a sampler made by Grandmother Grant at the age of 12, while she was in boarding school. The date on this sampler is as follows: "Se ed by Margaret McKinzie, Stornoway, Feb. 1808." Grandmother's education gave her an outstanding position in her community but did not prepare her for making a living. With the help of her sons, it became her duty to carry on the business as best she could.

The older children had been given the advantage of a good education, but the two youngest girls, Jessie and Jeanne, were deprived of this, acquiring what they could from the village school. The people of northern Scotland spoke Gaelic, but the schools taught English.

The McDonald family lived in the same village and the two families were close friends. The McDonalds were mechanical men and gardeners.

In this village, most men of Father's time became professional men, and I am convinced that his parents wished to prepare him in the same way. But Father was a restless boy who loved the people of the outdoors best. He was a friendly boy who was often asked to accompany the minister on his trips to the fishing villages where he made calls to christen the children.

At the age of 16 Father was sent to Edinburgh for an education. This would seem to be the opportunity of his life, but again that restless spirit demonstrated itself. The close confinement of the Edinburgh school became too restrictive for one who loved the out-of-doors, and he ran away and went to sea. He spent some years on trading vessels, going into ports of England, Welen, and those as far north as the midnight sun.

The Scotch have a penchant for nicknames, and Jeanne was known as Little Jane. Jane and John were engaged for a long time, for John had to save enough to establish a home and the Scotch reputation notwithstanding, saving money was not one of his virtues.

About three weeks before their wedding day the couple went to church together. Jane wore a black taffeta dress with a full skirt and tight bodice, with flowing sleeves that had an undersleeve of lace that was held tight at the wrist. With this she wore a taffeta lolman. At the regular morning service their betrothal was announced by the minister.

After the wedding, a dinner was served and presided over by Grandmother Grant. The wedding gown was cream India mull with a Dresden design, a costume that seems to be coming into vogue again. A cream-colored cashmere shawl accompanied the bride's costume. It also carried the Dresden design in the border. This dress is still a family possession.

Among the wedding presents were some heirlooms. These have been carefully treasured, and most of them are in the family still. A spinning wheel, the gift of a cabinet maker, was there, polished and ready for its venture into the new land.

The trip to America was delayed for two years on account of Grandfather McDonald's illness. After Grandfather's death, Grandmother McDonald decided to come to America also, as most of her family was either there or going. A sister of Father's, Mrs. George Frazier, bereft of her husband who was lost at sea off the coast of England, decided to join the company. She felt that she could give her three sons, William, Hector and Colen a better chance at life in America. Besides the new additions to the party, there was now a 6-month-old baby, William McDonald.

A memorandum kept by Father went as follows: John McDonald and family left Shieldaig, May 26, 1857, sailed from Liverpool, England, June 5, 1857. Arrived at New York July 8, 1857.

From New York the group traveled by train to Chicago, a small western village at that time. At Chicago they were met by Uncle Donald McDonald, and taken to Kewanes, where he and Aunt Ann had established a home some time before.

Father followed farming here, but did not purchase a permanent home. At this time there was a great emigration from the middle west to Oregon and Washington due to the passage of the congressional land grant bill, granting homesteads to settlers in these parts. Father and Mother had not been happy on the plains of Illinois. They missed the mountains of Scotland.

In May 1863 a company of friends started on the long journey for Oregon. Father placed his household things in one wagon. This wagon was guided by William Frazier, who had made his home with them since the time of his mother's death. He was 14 now. Father and the family occupied the second wagon.

This company was to join a caravan of 100 wagons at Omaha. At this time the Indians were particularly troublesome, so the train was conducted through the greater danger by a government escort of 36 mule teams and 150 men under the command of Captain Creaford.

This great cavalcade of immigrants and soldiers proved too formidable for the wandering bands of Indians to attack, and the settlers were permitted to pursue their course unmolested.

On October 5 the company entered the Grande Ronda Valley. So charmed were they with its beauty and possibilities that some of the company decided to call it home.

Instead of homesteading, Father bought a farm of 360 acres with a house, or cabin. This place, situated at the foot of the Indian trail near Mount Emily, with wooded background, a beautiful stretch of foreground meadow, and babbling streams running through it, was home for the McDonald family for many years.

Supplies for the first year must have come from Walla Walla, the older settlement. Then came the Rinehart gristmill and the Oliver sawmill. As soon as possible a new house was built. It was a log house, and Father hewed the logs. The sawmill supplied lumber for floors and additions. A fireplace in the sitting room and one in Mother's bedroom are places around which pleasant memories linger. When company came we were often shooed off to Mother's room after supper, where we were given special privileges. This was especially true when Uncle and Auntie Smith came, as they often did. They were delightful people, but were spiritualists, and they usually wandered off to spirit land before the evening was over. Mother thought theirs were not good bedtime stories for children.

Before the house was occupied by the family it was the poling place for the first election of that district.

The first homes were entirely on the edges of the valley where springs, streams, and meadow grass could be found. The rest of the valley was one waving sea of bunch grass. The grass, so called for the way it grew in bunches, grew four feet high or more. Stock could live out all winter, as there was always feed above the snow.

Father had a small flock of sheep, and here is the place for something more about the spinning wheel. Wool had to be washed, spun into yarn, then washed again and knitted into stockings, socks and mittens for this big family. Wool mattresses and wool comforters made good warm beds. Can you envision such a busy mother? The bur-r-r of the spinning wheel could be heard almost daily. Mother often kept a book beside the wheel, and when she became weary from spinning, she would relax by reading. Is it surprising that I associated the spinning wheel with the life of the family?

On winter evenings, the sitting room was where the family gathered; some with books, others with a checker or chess game. Later the whiz of ping pong could be heard from the dining room, and occasionally the sound of sleigh bells announced the arrival of friends who came for an evening. It took only a few people to add to our group to make a real party. For refreshments, popcorn, apples, cookies, or doughnuts were always on hand. Mother almost always served callers with tea and cake. If you should go to Scotland now, you would find that this custom still prevails.

You may wonder how this family got any education beyond the country school. Everyone was sent away for a time. The older ones to Blue Mountain University and perhaps business training in Portland. Duncan and Hector had two years at Bishop Scott. I had one year at Ascension, and one year at Pacific. It did not take a mint of money to do this or we probably would have been deprived of it. I know that some of the family would have loved to go farther had the purse been bigger.

In the 1880s, a lovely new home was built. Soon after this, the children began to go to homes of their own. The parents, though lonely, were philosophical enough to accept the inevitable and looked forward to frequent homecomings, when the house again rang with happiness and laughter.

Modern machinery for a time pushed the spinning wheel into oblivion. Then it was launched into a new career. As such, it made its first appearance accompanying "The Fast Spinning Song," sung by Ina Wright Herbet at the Stewart Opera House. Since that time it has been much in demand as a symbol of the industry and marvelous genius of pioneer mothers, whose uppermost thoughts were their love for home and family.

Emilie A. Bird
Beatrice, Nebraska

Great-Great-Grandson Resembles Ancestor

My great-grandfather, Corbulious Coates, was born in Yorkshire, England, on February 3, 1832. In those days, young men left the old countries at 18, when they had to register for the draft or army. He came to America when he was 17. The ship's passenger contract ticket is still in the family after 144 years.

When Corbulious first came to this country in 1849 he worked for other people. He took out his constitution or naturalization papers on March 26, 1855, and became a United States citizen at the age of 23. On October 31, 1861, he married Harriet Vasey, whose family also came from England.

Corbulious bought 318 acres of land, which is located at the east edge of Scott County in west central Illinois. In 1854 he purchased

140 acres for $2,640. Other purchases were made in 1864 and 1876. The family lived in a log cabin until their large eight-room northern colonial home was finished in 1871.

Corbulious died January 22, 1891, and Harriet died June 4, 1899. Both were buried in the Lynnville Cemetery. A son who died in infancy is also buried there. Corbulious and Harriet had two living sons, one of whom was my grandfather, and six living daughters. The farm was divided between the two sons. When my sister and I recently inherited the farm, we sold the house off the land to Glenn Robert Coates, a cousin, and wife Diane. Glenn is the great-great-grandson of Corbulious, and he looks like him, too.

> Patricia Rutherford
> Winchester, Illinois

A 99-Year Lease

We have our family history back to 1509. Sir Knight John Keay of Scotland has the record printed of a large tree that shows where Francis Scott Key came in; our record follows him. A legend handed down by the old Scotch says that they are descendants of the lost tribe of Israel and that in the early days of civilization—before the Norman conquest—they settled in a small country called Saxony. This country later fell into the hands of the Germans.

Unable to speak German, the Scotch began looking for another land to settle. They wanted hilly land with fertile valleys and streams. They found what they were looking for in what is now Scotland and settled there, scattering into Ireland, Wales and Lancashire, England. Most of those who came to America sailed out of Lancaster and landed in New York, then found their way into the southern states. The name Key has been spelled Kaey, Keay, Keys and Kee, but our lineage settled on the name Key. All the variations trace back to the ancient families of England and Scotland and the lineage of Sir Kaey, an ancient Briton and one of the knights of the warlike table of the noble Prince Arthur. In 1641, at the time of the Norman conquest, John Key was made a baronet. He was the first to spell the name Key. From the family's earliest history, it has been noted for its energy, pride, resourcefulness, initiative, mental ability, love of nature, courage and leadership.

The first name recorded in America was Thomas Key of Warwick River, Virginia, 1626. Seven Key brothers came from Scotland at about the time of the Revolutionary War. They took up land where the city of Brooklyn, New York, now stands. Later, they deeded this land away for 99 years and moved farther west. The 99-year term expired about 1870, but the Key brothers had failed to keep a complete family record and were unable to regain their property. The property, which comprises about five blocks on both Broadway and Fifth Avenues, was worth at least $200,000,000 several years ago.

Our Key family settled in Crawford County, Missouri, around Steelville. A new town nearby was named Keyville because most of the people in the area were named Key. On January 24, 1901, they decided to leave this area and move to a new land called the Oklahoma Territory, which did not have statehood until 1907. The families, along with farm animals, farm implements and household items, came by boxcar on the St. Louis and San Francisco Railroad line. They settled in Lincoln County at Chandler, about 40 miles from Oklahoma City.

Distinguished Key family members include: American lawyer and author of "The Star Spangled Banner" Francis Scott Key; English military historian Sir John William Key; British Admiral Sir Ashley Cooper Key; American jurist and cabinet officer David McKendar Key of Tennessee; and Swedish social writer Miss Ellen Key.

Whenever we meet a person named Key, they all go back to the story of the seven brothers leaving Scotland and the 99-year lease in Brooklyn.

Gladys Key Perry
Guymon, Oklahoma

A New Immigrant Was Born

Just recently I had the privilege of telling my teenage grand-nephew, Joshua, that his great-great-great-great-grandfather was also named Joshua. His ancestor was a Methodist "circuit-rider" during his life.

Joshua's wife had parents of Scotch descent, who sailed from Ireland to America in 1805. As these young parents traveled toward the United States, their baby daughter was born—aboard ship on the Atlantic Ocean! For these brave immigrants, maternity was no obstacle to their opportunity! I hope there was a fellow passenger capable of singing a lullaby while they were in motion on the ocean!

Hope Robinson
Yale, Iowa

Dad's Birthplace Was a "Castle"

My father, who was born in Scotland in 1876, came to this country around 1884. His father had been to the States several times, since he was a cattle buyer in Scotland and brought the cattle to America by ship to be sold to farmers here. After several trips the father decided to bring his family to America for a better life. The deciding factor seemed to be taxes, which were going up and up in Scotland.

Dad was 8 years old and had full run of the ship. Being a sociable kid, he got acquainted with many of the hired personnel who worked aboard. The thing he remembered most was following the steward, who hauled ashes from the furnaces below deck to the upper deck and dumped them over the railing into the ocean. Seeing those cinders and ashes fall the long distance made a lasting impression on him.

The family docked in Philadelphia, then made their way by train to southern Iowa, where there was already a settlement of Scotsmen. In later years Dad was the only one who ventured away from that area when he got old enough to be out on his own. He made his way to Missouri, met my mother, married and settled down on a scully lease until he could buy land of his own.

When the children came along his favorite saying was "I was born in a castle in Scotland." We would grin, and with tongue in cheek, say "Sure, sure."

It wasn't until 1977, 12 years after my father died, that my husband and I made a trip to Scotland to do some genealogy research. The map of Scotland that we were given listed a place called the Castle of Balzeordie. To make a long story short, it turned out to be the place where my dad was born. We went to see it. The place was a large stone house with probably 15 or 16 rooms in it. There was a courtyard in the back, with small apartments built in a "u" shape for servants' quarters.

Of course we were curious and began asking questions. We were told to go to a farm about a mile down the road, since that man had charge of renting the house and the grounds. We went.

A thrill went through me when we found that man. He knew my family name and remembered them when they lived in Scotland. We asked why the huge house was called a castle and he gave us the following story:

Away back in time, some members of the royal family were out hunting in this area. A severe storm came up, and some of the servants were sent to this farmhouse to ask if the prince and his entourage could stay for the night. Of course they were given permission. Ever since the place had been dubbed "The Castle."

So my dad was right. He was born in a castle—at least that is what he had always heard it called. Now we live with the guilt of making fun of him saying, "I was born in a castle."

If only we could reply, "Yes, Dad, we know you were born in a castle, and you are a member of royalty in our eyes!"

Zoe Rexroad
Adrian, Missouri

Family Sought Free-Thinking Society

A recent drive through The Amboys reminded me of family ties with the area.

In the late 1600s, a respected merchant by the name of Grimstone Boude left England to set up a new business in the then-thriving colonial seaport of Perth Amboy. Like many other entrepreneurs of his time, Grimstone was a free thinker, morally at odds with restrictive English laws.

In 1753, Mary Boude, daughter of Grimstone's son Thomas, married Matthew Clarkson of Philadelphia.

They had a son, David Clarkson, who went down to St. Kitts, British West Indies, in 1787 to establish and run a shipping business dealing in mahogany and rum. At St. Kitts, he courted Ann Amory. This couple opted to live out their lives in the islands.

In 1810, their daughter, Mary, became the wife of Isaac Prince, whom she met when he was U.S. Consul at St. Bartholomew, French West Indies. Isaac, a native of Basking Ridge, New Jersey, had business interests that eventually took them to live in Philadelphia.

Among their many offspring was a daughter, Sarah. In 1854, while visiting a sister in Astoria, Sarah met and married Edward Hewitt, a native New Yorker.

Sarah Prince Hewitt was my great-grandmother.

A century later life came full circle when I moved back to the Amboy area where Grimstone Boude began his New World odyssey—midway between New York and Philadelphia—thousands of miles from merry old England and The West Indies.

At times I wonder, if, somewhere out there, old Grimstone is observing the winding progression of things since he made the decision to leave England for Perth Amboy in quest of a more free-thinking society.

Sara Hewitt Riola
Lakewood, New Jersey

Uncovering an Interesting History

I am a seventh generation descendant of Thomas Cresap: pioneer, patriot and pathfinder, as he was known in Maryland. He was born at Skipton-In-Craven, Yorkshire, England, in 1694. As a lad of 15, he immigrated to the colony of Maryland around 1710. Little is known of his life until his marriage on April 30, 1727, to a spirited lady named Hannah Johnson. They first lived near Havre de Grace, Maryland. They were the parents of seven children, five of whom lived to maturity. Four of them had descendants.

In 1740, Cresap purchased land on the Maryland side of the Potomac River. Here he built a stockade home-fort, later named Oldtown, in a beautifully scenic area. Here he continued his trading enterprises, buying and selling land and surveying. His location became a crossroads, and as parties of Indians passed by, he fed them and provided supplies for their expeditions. They called him "Big Spoon." Cresap became a colonel in the Maryland Militia, and was one of the founders of the Sons of Liberty, the first patriotic society in America. He served with Braddock and Washington and surveyed their trail over the Allegheny Mountains in 1751. Traders, missionaries, and soldiers were also recipients of his generosity. His sons were Daniel Cresap, for whom Dan's Mountain is named; Thomas Jr., killed in a battle with the Indians on Savage Mountain in 1757; and Michael, captain in Lord Dunsmore's War in 1774 and First Captain of the Maryland Rifle Company in 1775, marching to Boston. He died of a fever shortly after that conflict. Three grandsons served as captain and lieutenants in Dunsmore's and the Revolutionary War.

How did I find this famous ancestor? By a stroke of luck just a few years ago. My mother kept a journal of family names and dates. I knew that one of my father's sisters was named Myrtle Cresap Carlile. I had no idea who she was named for until one day in 1988, when I met a newly admitted patient in the hospital where I worked. Her last name was Cresap. She was my source for a hard-back book published in 1987, *The History of the Cresaps*, by

Bernarr Cresap and Joseph Ord Cresap. My great-grandparents, Alexander S. and Ellen Cresap Carlisle, were listed with their six children. I soon discovered a number of Cresap cousins in the area and was privileged to attend the 1991 Diamond Jubilee Reunion of the Cresap Society, held in Cumberland, Maryland. Cousins from all over the country attended for a weekend of fellowship, a planned luncheon and banquet with special speakers and musical programs. There was free time to visit all of the landmarks—the homesite of Thomas Cresap, museums, cemeteries—to take a ride over the Old National Road, and to visit Oldtown. My second reunion, in 1993, was even more interesting. What a thrill to discover a family that was such a part of our American history.

Mary Carlile Ruhs
Hamilton, Illinois

Cheers for the Pioneer Spirit

My husband's great-grandmother, Lady Marcell O'Brien, from Cork County, Ireland, fell in love with the stable hand, John Keenan, and they were excommunicated to America. They were married just before embarking for America, but they forgot their marriage license and returned to get it. In doing so, they missed their boat. As the story goes, this ship and all aboard were lost at sea. They took the next ship to America and settled near Freeport, Illinois, where they became the parents of three boys. Great-Grandfather was killed in a thrashing accident. Great-Grandmother remarried and brought her family to Paola, Kansas, where they bought a farm from Chief Baptiste Peoria on the Marais des Cygnes River near Henson, Kansas.

We have much to thank our pioneer relatives for—their courage and persistence gave us our rich heritage today.

The Plummers
Osawatomie, Kansas

Eight Generations of Fifields

William Fifield was the first family ancestor to come to America. He arrived in April 1643 during the "great migration." He was aboard the *Hercules*. His sympathies were with the Puritans. He came in bondage to the ship's captain or owner, paid the debt of his passage, and was declared a freeman in 1641. He moved to Hampton, New Hampshire, with a group that settled the town. He married; his wife's name was Mary. The town of Hampton was the family home for many generations. William was a constable, selectman (a town council representative) and an attorney, or barrister. Many of his descendants were doctors, teachers, ministers and attorneys. William and Mary both lived long lives.

William's son Benjamin was killed by Indians. There were other family members who suffered the same fate. It was the custom to pay a bounty for an Indian skull or scalp when it was shown in court. If they were killed during an attack $75 was paid and divided among the heirs and wife. The Indians learned to scalp their victims from the white man.

Captain Edward and Ensign John Fifield, brothers, went to sea. They carried on commerce along the Atlantic coast and with England. Some Fifields were fishermen, others were in the navy. Fifields also fought in the Revolutionary War. They served at the battles of Bennington and Bunker Hill. Sewell Fifield was a famous fifer in the old state militia of New Hampshire.

A line of Fifield ancestors lived near Daniel Webster and his relatives in New Hampshire. Webster wrote that he had seen seven generations in the Fifield house; there were actually eight. A woman who married into the Fifield family attended Daniel Webster's birth.

The Fifields and Websters were schoolmates. Ebenezer Fifield attended Salisbury Academy and entered Dartmouth College with Ezekiel Webster, studying medicine with Dr. Nathan Smith of Hanover. When Daniel Webster went to Boston to study, Ebenezer went with him and completed his studies with Dr. Asa Ballard.

The young men boarded together. On completion of his studies Dr. Fifield went to Maine, but then returned to Boston.

In the War of 1812, Dr. Fifield joined the navy and became a surgeon on a ship of war. The vessel was captured by the French and taken to France. He was a prisoner for eight months; his health was shattered when he returned to Boston.

He taught in an academy, and later was a principal in another school. He took a job in the old State Bank until his eyesight failed.

Althea Fifield Kendall
Pullman, Washington

Grandmother Never Mentioned Regrets

The question continues to haunt the minds of her descendants. Was she born with a congenital predisposition to depression? Or did she have a great deal to be depressed about?

Kate Margaret was born in 1847 in Wyke Regis, county of Dorsetshire, England, the second in a family of 11 children. They were socially prominent people; her father owned a grocery business and bakery. As Kate grew up, she helped out in the business as bookkeeper and clerk. She was vivacious and fun loving. Through the years the tale has been told that she raced a horse against a train. She was adventuresome, too, which probably led to her later problems.

On a nearby farm, a young man was growing up who soon found more and more excuses to go to either the store or the bakery.

His and Kate's friendship developed into love, and in 1873 the young couple was married in the great old Episcopal church in Wyke Regis.

The young groom was adventuresome, too, and very soon the two told their families that they had decided to set sail for America.

If Kate could have foreseen the nearly three weeks of dreadful seasickness during which she almost died, she may have reconsidered the decision that changed their lives forever.

She lived to arrive in pre-Ellis Island New York. From there they took a train to Buffalo, where they boarded a ship that was supposed to carry them on The Great Lakes to Duluth, Minnesota.

A little black cloud seemed to hover over them, because the ship broke down. A second ship also broke down. All the time she was on the water, the young bride had the queasiness in her stomach reminiscent of the ocean voyage.

The third ship carried them to Duluth, where they took the train to an area east of Moorhead, Minnesota.

Being used to the finer things in life, living in a shanty with Indians peering in the windows soon brought tears from Kate. She had never seen Indians before, and though they seemed mostly friendly, their presence still frightened her.

Even though she loved her husband desperately, Kate was homesick. And try as she might, it was increasingly hard to hold back her tears. Finally it became virtually impossible. She was unhappy in her new home, and her memories of their terrible journey across the Atlantic made her realize that she could never endure the trip back to her homeland.

At last, the young husband, with problems of his own trying to farm the land, took his bewildered bride to an older woman in the village of Hawley. There Kate had someone to talk to, someone who understood when Kate had morning sickness. Mrs. Chant spent hours listening to the young woman verbalize her feelings.

A baby girl, Blanche Eliza, was born in that home. She was only 6 weeks old when the family of three moved to a primitive home on the land George had acquired by pre-emption. Gradually the hard-working farmer provided his family with a six-room house on the prairie—a mansion in those days.

Four more children were born: Rose, Kate (my mother), Charles and young George. It must have bothered my grandmother to see her children attend a one-room school, instructed by a teacher who had barely finished eight grades herself. Kate had been able to attend a private school in England.

Did she ever regret having left home and family to venture to a new land? She never said so. But she often mentioned the nightmarish trip across the bouncing waves of the Atlantic.

As the children grew and married, George prospered as a farmer. He built a two-story home in Hawley, where they retired.

The one time I saw Grandmother, when I was 5 or 6, she was bedridden and sent my mother to fetch a doll from a cupboard. It was the only gift I remember receiving from her, but in receiving it, I understood she loved me.

I admire her for her courage and determination. She was one of many hardy pioneers.

> Mary Gaylord
> Balsam Lake, Wisconsin

A Strong Foundation of Faith

My great-grandmother came from England via that hungry ocean. Freshly butchered cows provided beef stew for everyone on board. They estimated how many more days of travel were left before reaching shore by how much meat was consumed. They drank gallons of tea for their liquid pleasure and comfort.

Still energetic after reaching the coast, they purchased horses and wagons, loaded their few possessions and drove away to settle in many areas. Great-Grandmother married a Scotchman. They named their first daughter Matilda. Matilda grew up and married my Granddad Grimes, who was of Scotch-Irish descent. He was a preacher in the Arkansas Ozarks. I'm thankful for the deep faith in God that he preached about, which is still alive in our families. To this family four children were born. The oldest was my mother, Matilda Jane Grimes. She grew into adulthood and married my dad. They had six children, including me, Matilda Jane. By 1912 my folks had bought acres and built a farmhouse in Kansas. We lived five miles from Damar, which was a French settlement, and four miles from Nicodemus, a black settlement. Each August 1 the Emancipation Proclamation was honored. Nine miles from Webster and 20 miles from Stockton was the seat of Rooks County. Webster is now the location of a state lake and recreation center.

My memory flies through pages of untouched photographs, more than enough to fill a big book. I'm the only Matilda Jane still alive. For my English ancestry and our deep faith and belief in God, for good beef stew, for all the chats and cups of hot tea, thanks!

I am grateful for all of my nephews, nieces and cousins. England gave us generations of real day-to-day "spice." Life is precious.

Matilda Winters Cardin
Englewood, Colorado

First Nantucket Deed Still in Family

For a supposedly staid people, the British have a way with names. Starbuck is a prime example. The origin is obscure. Some say it comes from an ancient Norse word meaning "great man." Others claim it is a derivative of "Starbeck," a swamp in Nottinghamshire, England. In either case, the first Starbuck seems to have been one Richard Johnson, who, in the 14th century, felt there were too many sons of John for comfort. Not wanting to be one of the crowd, he elected to strike out on his own ... as a Starbuck.

In 1636, Edward Starbuck, with his wife, Katherine, and two small children left Leicestershire, England, for the colonial area that is now known as Dover, New Hampshire.

Around 1640, Edward was appointed a "wearesman" or official river fisherman. Wearesmen were required to supply the town and its church from their catches. He also served in the Massachusetts Legislature from 1643 to 1646. In 1647, having received permission to erect a sawmill, Edward went into the lumber business.

In 1659, at odds with the Puritans over the age at which baptism should be performed—an Anabaptist, he preferred baptism of adults, not children—Edward began looking for new horizons to conquer. This quest took him and other Alto, Wisconsin, dissidents by open boat to Nantucket, an island 18 miles off Cape Cod. After spending the winter there, Edward traveled to Dover and returned with his and 10 other families. He built a house at the head of Hummock Pond, on land deeded to him by the Indians. That deed is the oldest original Nantucket document still in existence today.

Sara Hewitt Riola
Lakewood, New Jersey

They Burned the Feather Tick

My Grandpa Brown was born in England in the early 1800s. I don't know why he was being raised by an uncle, but the man was so cruel to him that he ran away at the age of 8. Through the help of a family to which he was apprenticed to learn a trade, he took care of himself from then on.

Grandpa outlived two wives with whom he had three sons before marrying a much younger Welsh girl. His sons and their small daughter came with him to America and settled near Junction City, Kansas. Later, they moved to a farm nearly 20 miles east, which is still in the hands of a direct descendent.

The only thing I ever remember hearing my mother tell about the trip to America was that the family brought with them a feather tick, which they were allowed to spread on the deck of the ship for sleeping. When my grandmother died of tuberculosis, after bearing at least seven more children, the doctor ordered them to burn the feather tick.

Marjorie Crouch
Uvalde, Texas

MY FOLKS AND THE LAND OF OPPORTUNITY

Relative Was a Revolutionary Soldier

Leaving Ireland in 1767, two brothers, William and Thomas Shanley, landed in Charleston, South Carolina, then a colony named Charles Town.

The older brother, William, who was 15 years old, received 150 acres: 100 for himself and 50 as parents' right for his younger brother, Thomas, who was under 15. The land was given as bounty for coming to the new land. It is located in Abbeville County, South Carolina.

My Great-Great-Great-Grandfather Thomas later served in the American Revolutionary War. He also had the distinction of being listed in the first U.S. Census for South Carolina, which was published in 1789 or 1790.

Janice I. Kinman
Carthage, Missouri

Descendant Proud of Family Legacy

My Great-Great-Grandfather John Bellaire, and his wife, Priscilla, left Eastgate, England, with their 1-year-old son, John Vincent, and landed on the shores of America in 1851. The transition from their homeland to America caused the young couple many hardships. The long trip was rough for my ancestors, who had very few possessions. The decision to leave their families and embark on a new venture was a painful experience. They dreamed of a bright future for themselves and their child.

Great-Great-Grandpa settled with his family in Indiana, near the Michigan border, to work for a farmer. Priscilla's frail body weakened; she was homesick for relatives left behind in England. One year after arriving in America, Priscilla died. Her husband, heartbroken and in despair, placed his son in the loving care of the Ned Gray family in Michigan, a few miles from his home. John Vincent grew to manhood and took up farming as his father and adoptive parents had done.

John Vincent married Agnes VanAntwerp, a native of Holland, and to this union were born 10 children. One was my grandmother, Rose Bellaire, who married Albert Reed. After my Great-Grandfather Bellaire was widowed he lived with my Grandma Reed. I loved the old gentleman dearly. I couldn't understand how he could drink hot tea and not get his white mustache wet. One morning under my close observation he explained the separate section on his cup; sharing the secret took away the mystery. He always told about my ancestors. When he died it was a terrible loss.

My ancestors left a rich legacy for their descendants. I'm proud of my brave and determined ancestors. I inherited their strength and courageous ability to meet tough obstacles, and I now pass those traditions on to my great-grandson. America, the Land of Opportunity. I'm so very proud to be an American.

Phyllis M. Peters
Three Rivers, Michigan

"His Fighting Age Was 48"

Vincent Hawkins was a native of England, born in Derbyshire in July 1800. He came to America and located in Pennsylvania, where he was married to Annie Crowell, a Maryland native. He enlisted at the first call for troops at the beginning of the 1861 rebellion. He was 61. When asked his age, he said his fighting age was 48. He served his term of three years and then returned home. He enlisted again a few months later in Cleveland, Ohio, in the 413th Ohio Infantry. He remained there until the close of the Civil War, when he was discharged from the invalid corps. In 1873 he visited his son and family in southern Minnesota; he died a few weeks later. He was my husband's great-grandfather.

Erma Hawkins
Tucson, Arizona

Stowaways Witnessed Momentous Years in America

The cold Atlantic Ocean must have seemed a minor obstacle to Cullen Thomas Conly, who dreamed of a promised new life on the shores of Georgia in 1836. The 16-year-old Irish lad was escaping to a new land—one where he would carve a life for himself free from economic and religious oppression, overcrowding and famine.

Born in 1820, near Mount Conly in County Antrim, Ireland, the courageous and adventuresome lad managed to stow himself away on a freighter anchored in nearby Glenarm Harbor. He remained undetected by the ship's officers until they reached the harbor of Savannah, Georgia. The ship's captain refused to let him go ashore at Savannah and planned to return the lad to Ireland; however, the night before the ship was scheduled to return to Ireland, Cullen jumped overboard and swam ashore.

What made the Irish lad, who would become my great-great-grandfather, sever all ties with his past and never return to his homeland? What made him hide on a ship and journey 3,000 miles across a treacherous ocean to an unknown land? Did he know that the land, climate, people, houses, food and clothing were different from those of his native Ireland? Did he leave because of daring and love of adventure, or was he obsessed with the desire to better his economic condition? Perhaps this young Irish Protestant was fleeing the religious conflict between the Catholics and Protestants that has divided the Emerald Isle for generations.

It is not known what the first eight years in America held for this determined immigrant, but he must have possessed unusual courage and will power to cope with the problems he faced on arriving in Georgia—finding work to pay for his food, clothing, and shelter while at the same time adjusting to a strange new country filled with vast forests and miles of unoccupied lands—a quite different place from the land of his birth.

The next record of Cullen Thomas was in 1844, in Houston County, Georgia—200 miles away from Savannah—where he married Dicy Talton. He was 24 and she was 19. Shortly after their marriage, Cullen and Dicy joined the westward movement toward Texas—the land of abundant opportunity and wide-open spaces. Journeying overland in wagons, on horseback and on foot, people from Georgia, South Carolina, Tennessee, Alabama and Mississippi began to migrate west to the land of promise.

Louisiana was the eastern gateway to Texas, and the hill section of north Louisiana was being settled in the 1830s and 1840s. The rolling upland of the northern half of Louisiana reminded the immigrants of the hills of Georgia, Alabama and Carolina. The hills were interspersed with beautiful streams fed by many sparkling springs. The rivers and bayous offered an economical transportation and travel network, but most of all, a way to move the products of forest and field to market at New Orleans, where the produce intermingled with world trade. The forests abounded in wild game such as deer, bear, turkey, ducks, geese, squirrels, quail, and numerous fur-bearing animals: raccoon, opossum, mink, otter, weasel and rabbits. The streams were stocked with many species of fish, and alligators were abundant. The fertile soil, combined with these other factors, led the immigrants to decide that this was the paradise they were seeking. They did not go on to Texas, but settled instead in northern Louisiana.

Cullen Thomas, his bride, and a few of her relatives settled on the east bank of Lake Bistineau in Bienville Parish, near the present town of Ringgold, Louisiana, where the first of their 10 children was born. They built a cabin, cleared the land for farming, and raised six sons and four daughters. A religious man with a closely knit family, his 10 children all remained nearby, acquiring land and farming it.

In 1859, the Ireland-born immigrant became a naturalized citizen of the United States, 16 years after landing on its shores.

Unlike many Irish immigrants, who came to America and worked as street sweepers, ditch diggers or other common laborers,

Cullen Thomas was a farmer. By 1861 he had acquired around 580 acres of land and owned and operated a cotton gin and a gristmill.

He was 41 years old when the Civil War began. A number of men that age joined the Confederate forces, although some southerners were exempt from military service if they operated a gin and their number of children was sufficient reason for not joining the army. There is no evidence that Cullen Thomas requested exemption, although it was alleged that he did not believe in slavery and owned no slaves. After the war was over, he registered to vote in 1867.

Although he adapted to a new way of life in America, Cullen Thomas retained some Irish ideals and customs. He meticulously looked after his possessions and kept the most detailed records of his income and expenditures. He was frugal and the master of his household, and, true to his Irish descent, he occasionally enjoyed a drink of good whiskey. He was reared to provide with his own hands as many creature comforts as possible, which served him well on the semi-frontier.

Thus he spent the 27 years of his life in Louisiana. Those were momentous years in the history of our nation as well as the crowning years of a short, but good, life. In 1872, at the age of 52, Cullen Thomas Conly died in Bienville Parish, leaving behind 10 children and 83 grandchildren—42 grandsons and 41 granddaughters. In 1976 there were more than 1,700 descendants of the Conly lad who stowed away on a ship and came to America for a better life.

Leta Leshe
Shreveport, Louisiana

A New Bride for the Homestead

The immigration story of my grandparents, Robert and Mary Anne McClean, was really a tale of love, romance and success.

Grandpa Robert lived at Moys of Castleshane in County Monaghan, North Ireland. On their small farm they raised flax and potatoes and grazed sheep. His was a family of seven boys and two girls. He was the second oldest son.

In Ireland, only the oldest son would inherit the land. So the younger boys worked in the peat bogs down south. Robert loved the land and wanted to own his own someday, but in Ireland there was no land available to buy. He would have to leave Ireland. On April 10, 1869, he and his younger brother, John, did just that. They set sail from Liverpool on the good ship *Idaho*, with hopes of high adventure and a very distant dream of someday owning a farm in far-off America.

They went to the newly formed village of Wahoo, Nebraska, where they had cousins. Robert got a job running the ferry owned by James Lee, his cousin. Brother John worked for another cousin, H.J. Lee, who owned a hardware store in Wahoo.

Robert enjoyed running the ferry across the Platte River between Saunders and Dodge counties. He could see the possibility of homesteading when he could earn some money. But what would a homestead be without a wife and family? He remembered an Irish lass with dancing blue eyes back home. He saved every penny carefully, and in 1871, with a stroke of very good luck, he had the means to go back across the sea to win his Irish sweetheart, Mary Anne Carson. On March 26, 1872, they were married at her home in Harrymount by her uncle, Rev. James Carson.

In a short time they set sail for America, bringing with them Robert's brother James, and sister Eliza McClean Birnie, her husband, John, and their four young children.

Grandpa and Grandma·homesteaded about a mile and a half northwest of Wahoo. Grandpa Robert's dream had come true: a wife and a home on land he could call his own!

Dorothy (McClean) Boettner
Fremont, Nebraska

A Stop on the Underground Railroad

My story comes from data I obtained about my mother's grand-parents. Her grandfather was George Menown Watt. He was born in 1807 in Belfast, Ireland, and came to America in 1821 at the age of 14. The family consisted of George, his wife, nine children and Aunt Rose. It took them six weeks to cross the Atlantic Ocean in a sailing vessel. They experienced severe hardships, and soon after arriving the three older girls died from the effects of exposure.

George Menown Watt was a nephew of James Watt, who invented steam power in Glasgow, Scotland. George Watt married Jane Findly McClelland in 1838. Her father was Captain McClelland, a veteran of the War of 1812. He had been commissioned to commander under General Harrison during the Black Hawk War. He had many different assignments.

After he completed his service to his country he returned to his family. He was twice married and fathered 20 children.

With his enterprising nature, Captain McClelland became interested in silk manufacturing in Green County, Ohio. Near his home he erected a small building to house the silkworms. It had shelves placed one above the other, far enough apart to place mulberry branches upon which the silkworms fed. These branches were cut from mulberry trees, of which he had planted about five acres. The branches were gathered and placed by his son Sam and grandson Simon Jolly. The branches had to be replaced as fast as the leaves were eaten off.

When the worms matured and made their cocoons, these cocoons were gathered, scalded and placed in glass tumblers, with a certain number in each glass container and a number of glasses in each group. A fine thread from each cocoon was joined together with that from another cocoon, until silk thread of the desired size was made.

His wife and older daughters did the spinning and spooling on wheels made just for that purpose. There was a ready market for silk because it was so scarce at this time. On one occasion enough silk thread was sent to be woven for a dress for his wife, Martha. When it came back it was a beautiful dark green color. It was probably the first "homegrown" silk dress in Green County.

Captain McClelland, being of strict faith, was religiously opposed to slavery. He was often suspected of aiding slaves' escapes by means of the underground railroad, the secret route from one sympathizer to another, usually traveled at night. McClelland's sons were choppers and cleared land for their father. As they trimmed brush from the trees they piled it into huge piles, higher than a house; some of these piles had pits under them where the slaves were hidden. The small boys carried food and messages to the hidden slaves for their father and played in the woods all the time just to keep a lookout for spies.

On one occasion Captain McClelland learned government spies were coming to search his premises. He prepared by sending extra provisions and a warning to the slaves to be ready to move on at a moment's notice. The spies came and searched the buildings with McClelland following, a gun in his belt. When they finished their search, there was one place they had failed to look, the large fireplace, where a fire was burning. They refused to look there, so he drew his gun on them and told them to look. While the flames were dying down and keeping the spies occupied in the house, the slaves were spirited away to their next stop by his sons, Jack, Robert and Isiah. No further attempt was ever made to search the McClelland's surroundings.

Captain McClelland was a member of the Second United Presbyterian Church at Xenia, Ohio, at the time of his death on April 13, 1846. All his life he strived for a happy life by doing good deeds for others. He was a great addition to the large Watt family.

Grace B. Horner
Junction City, Kansas

Life in the New State of Wisconsin

My great-grandparents, John and Rebecca, came to western Wisconsin in 1868. The only transportation option from Stillwater, Minnesota, to St. Croix Falls, Wisconsin, was the packet boats. Their oxen, oxcarts, hay and feed, tools and all of their personal belongings were on the lower deck of the riverboat, *The Nellie Kent.*

John Lumsden and Rebecca Densmore had emigrated from Scotland several years before and were married in Nova Scotia. Then they moved to Ontario. They must have had a very strong desire to come to the United States. Perhaps they heard of land in Polk County, Wisconsin: almost the entire county was once owned by General Caleb Cushing, a Civil-War-veteran-turned-land-speculator. In 1868 he was involved in Massachusetts politics, but he was also the president of the Great European-American Emigration Land Company. His advertisements were probably instrumental in convincing people to settle in Wisconsin.

First they traveled by boat on Lake Huron, then by riverboats on the Illinois, Mississippi and St. Croix Rivers. At the time, these hardy souls had two sons, ages 13 and 5, a daughter, who would become my grandmother, 10, and a baby girl only 6 weeks old. Great-Grandmother must have been very brave to attempt such a trip, but she probably didn't have a choice in the matter.

Four families traveled together to settle in the same area. When they arrived at St. Croix Falls, Wisconsin, they went by oxcart north along the St. Croix River to where they were homesteading. They lived in tents while the four families helped one another build log cabins. Two of the men had been there the winter before, but the ground, covered with snow, didn't show its poor condition. They'd gone back to Ontario and said, "There's plenty of land." In time they discovered that the land was not rich and fertile in that location. That area today is known as "The Barrens." The sandy soil is okay for producing jack pine, but not for farming. The families moved a few miles to the southeast, where the soil is a rich loam.

Life must have been very hard in the new state of Wisconsin—the little towns were not nearby. Timber had to be cut for new houses and firewood, which was needed for warmth in the dreadfully cold winters. They raised sheep and carded and spun wool. They knitted mittens, sweaters, stockings and socks. They had to make candles and soap and bake bread; clothes had to be scrubbed on a washboard.

When they went to a town to buy flour, sugar, material and other necessities such as kerosene, nails, and tools, they used their trusty ox team and oxcart. It was a long day's trip.

Lucille Anton
Circle Pines, Minnesota

Unfavorable First Impressions

Dark murky water churned 'round the ship as it slowly headed out on its journey across the Atlantic. Hoping for a last glimpse of the emerald English countryside, I stood on deck, clinging to the guardrail while scanning the view. All I could see was the Southampton dockyard, with its outline of tall cranes and other ships in port. As the dismal grey sight receded, a loudspeaker bellowed instructions for passengers to stay in their cabins as we headed into a storm.

The cabin was lined with narrow bunks intended for servicemen's wives. Three other women occupied these bunks. A small central floor space contained a crib for my 10-month-old son, leaving barely enough room to stand and turn around. As the pitching of the ship increased, I soon learned to balance by planting my feet apart and rolling with the motion.

Ferocious winds and mountainous waves relentlessly battered our vessel as it tossed and rolled. Rising and dipping, we rose to the crest of huge walls of water only to plunge down, then up to the next. Most of the crew and passengers were seasick. Daily fire drills became our only exercise. We grasped handrails along the gangways and desperately clung to cold iron ladders while climbing between decks. After days of battering, a short lull between storms made it possible to go up on deck.

The bitter, salty wind stung my face and turned my cheeks apple red. Reclining in a sturdy, slatted wooden deck chair, I gazed at the azure horizon where sky met ocean. The sun glinted on choppy waves in the never-ending sea. From the clouds in the sky to the angry water to the rising and falling of the deck, all was motion.

The only distraction from the monotony of sea and sky was spotted midway on our journey. The loudspeaker announced that a ship could be seen passing on the horizon about five miles away.

The storm returned with a vengeance and was with us for the next week, until we finally arrived in New York on January 23, 1956.

FIRST IMPRESSIONS

New York was a bustling city filled with people who hated each other. Taxi drivers yelled obscenities, people pushed as they rushed by and hotel rooms had rows of locks on each door. All this was in stark contrast to the Kentish people and a countryside of green meadows and blossoming orchards. New York was a place to leave as quickly as possible. We left in an old blue Willys that we prayed would carry us to our destination.

As the scenery rushed by on this long, straight highway, I was astonished to see rundown houses with large cars in front and TV antennas on the roofs. The road seemed endless. With only a few stops along the way for bread, milk and cheese, we drove through New Jersey, Maryland, Virginia, North and South Carolina, Georgia and finally arrived in Orange Springs, Florida.

As the old Willys chugged to a stop in front of a small grocery store, I looked around in dismay. Once-white paint was peeling off weathered wood siding; faded signs were barely legible even in the bright Florida sun. Beside the entrance stood a rusty and dented cold drink cooler with 5 cents printed on it. Scruffy men slouched on benches near the cooler, chewing tobacco.

A short, sprightly old woman ran from her overgrown jungle of a garden across the street and introduced herself.

"I'm Miss Mary," she exclaimed. "You'll have to excuse my appearance, I've been picking blackberries."

Getting out of the car, my high heels sank into the sand. While extending my hand, I saw the remains of past meals dribbled down the woman's flour-sack dress. Declining an invitation for 'possum dinner, I waited to see where we would go.

The townspeople gathered in front of the store to meet me. Not understanding my English accent, they asked each other what language I was speaking. I slowed my speech to their southern drawl. They gradually began to understand me, and I was bombarded with questions.

"Do they have TV in England?"

"What 'bout 'frigerators?"

"Where is England?"

"Is it in Russia?"

It was decided that we should go to the only other store to find a place to stay. We rented a one-room cabin built of rough-sawn cypress, containing a bed, table, chair and hot plate. Water was obtained from an outside faucet. For $10 a month, this little cabin became our first home in the United States.

When we were able to afford $30 a month in rent, we moved into a large house that had probably been a fine home during the Civil War. Unused for years, it was in disrepair. The walls and ceiling were covered with small holes, but I was happy to be in a house with a kitchen, bathroom, bedroom and living room. As we moved in, I kept wondering about the mysterious holes in the plaster. Falling into bed exhausted after a day of cleaning, I finally discovered what made them. As I gazed at the ceiling, rats peered through the holes. I jumped out of bed in revulsion and ran to the kitchen. When I turned on the light, roaches scurried away from the brightness.

Our next home was a pest-free garage apartment in which the lumber was rotting. This home lasted until my first hurricane. The building swayed all night but remained upright.

We were finally able to purchase some $50-an-acre property, where we lived in a small trailer while building our home. Each payment for doing odd jobs bought material for the house. Our groceries were what we grew, gleaned from the woods or obtained on credit at the general store.

MONTANA

Almost 40 years have passed since my early impressions. The extreme poverty is only a distant memory. I now write from a comfortable log home in the scenic Bitterroot Valley. This is the Land of Opportunity. It is my home.

Brenda East
Victor, Montana

Chapter Two: Of Scandinavian Descent

Frugal to the End

My Swedish immigrant ancestor, Gus Johnson, arrived in New York City Harbor in September 1881. They could not disembark until President Garfield's funeral was over. Whales were sighted during the trip and the passengers nearly capsized the ship rushing to one side to observe them.

According to stories he told family members, children were allowed one pair of leather shoes a year. He wore his when he should have been more careful and was left with nothing but wooden shoes to wear. His sister, who was about his age, went to Sunday School and met Gus close to the church, where they exchanged shoes. He continued to church and she, wearing his wooden shoes, went home.

His mother made cheese for the family. It was stored in a manure pile to "ripen." No doubt it was good, but I can not eat Limburger cheese because of the smell. Every Christmas Grand-dad Johnson bought a large round of cheddar cheese. He also enjoyed his salted herring, which was soaked and poached for yuletime.

Genealogy records for Gus are scarce. He celebrated his 20th birthday on the ocean coming to America. I think I have found the passenger list, which listed Gus as six years older than his actual age. A genealogical friend assured me he would add to his age if he were going to a foreign land. He was also listed as Aaron Johnson, but officials in New York City told him it was not a Christian name, so he took his brother's name—spelled Gust—on his naturalization papers. I wonder if it wasn't on purpose to escape compulsory military service. We will never know.

Granddad settled in Illinois, where he worked for a Swedish farmer. He met my grandmother, who had an English background, when she came to work for the same Swedish family. After a period of time he had a choice of some acres or money and two horses. It is no wonder that, after being in this country for 11 years, he took the horses and money and married my grandmother. Later they moved near Independence, Kansas. Some of my earliest memories of visiting their home are of Grandmother reading the *Independence Reporter, Capper's Weekly,* and *The Weekly Kansas City Star* to Granddad as they sat in their yard in the evening, resting from their daily work.

In 1925 my parents bought a Model T touring car. As a Christmas present they took Granddad and Grandmother Johnson to Poteau, Oklahoma, to see a daughter who had been spoiled as a youngster. Whipped cream was her favorite. Grandmother took two half gallons of the night's cream when we left early in the morning. What a trip! Mother, Dad and my year-old sister in the front seat, my grandparents and three boys, the oldest not 6, in the back. Wrap robes kept us warm. Highways weren't marked as they are today, and they were gravel for the most part. We were on the wrong road three times. The last time we were nearly in Ft. Smith, Arkansas, before finding out we were not on our way to Poteau. Grandmother was getting weary and kept saying we would have butter by the time we arrived. Sure enough we did!

Granddad was not accustomed to modern facilities. Every day when nature called he cranked the Ford up and went out to the country where he could perform his "chores." He was very frugal.

In November 1945, when I returned from two years overseas, I took my fiancée to meet Granddad. Where was he? That 85-year-old man was out in the kafir cornfield with a gunnysack, pail and butcher knife, cutting off the heads of the kafir that had been missed by the combine. That is my last memory of my Swedish granddad, who passed away the following April, timidly complaining to the end that he could not go to the outdoor toilet.

Merle W. Austin
Collinsville, Oklahoma

A Sewing Machine for a Sweetheart

Soren Christian Anderson was from Vraa, Denmark. He came to Boston, Massachusetts, in 1872. After working there for awhile he traveled to Atlantic, Iowa. There he secured an agency for selling Singer sewing machines. He did well at this, but he really wished to be a farmer. He knew the government was giving away homestead land, but if he took some he wanted it to be good, fertile soil. He and a friend, A.P. Clemenson, decided to walk across the available land so they could choose what they wanted. They walked north into Dakota Territory and found good land with no rocks or stones in it. But they did not settle on it right away. They began walking westward, always on the watch for Indians. Several times they hid from Indian bands and then continued on their journey. After some months they arrived in Reno, Nevada. They were broke. Work was easily found there and they stayed for nearly two years. When they left they were able to get a train back to Iowa.

Soren married his sweetheart, Dorthea Mauritsen, and presented her with a Singer sewing machine, which is still in our family.

In 1882 Soren decided to take up a homestead. He thought the best land that was left was near Conde, in Dakota Territory. He filed on a claim and moved into a sod house that same year. He lived on that homestead and added four more quarter sections to it before his death in 1934.

Eunice Hoien Dahlgren
Sweet Home, Oregon

Life in the Land of Milk and Honey

They called the United States the "Land of Milk and Honey," but soon found out it wasn't all roses. My folks came from Norway in the early 1900s. My dad came first with another brother for their new adventure in America. They settled in Minnesota, working at various jobs for awhile to make a few dollars. Soon they were anxious to go to North Dakota and homestead. My dad lived in a one-room shack for several years until he could get a piece of land, as did his brother. After buying a few acres, my dad got ahold of a few horses, cows, etc. and started a very small farming operation.

A few years went by before he met a beautiful young lady who later would become my dear mother. She came to the United States all alone from the beautiful country of Norway. She said good-byes to her dad and sister, never to see them again. She sailed on a ship for three weeks, never knowing anybody and seasick much of the way. She did take her harmonica with her, and when she got too lonesome she'd go to her little cubbyhole room and play a few tunes. She was so musical and sang all the time. In Norway, she, her dad and sister always sang in a big choir. Perhaps that's why her six children were all musical, playing and entertaining in numerous places.

When she arrived in New York after sailing for three weeks, she got panicky. She couldn't speak English and really never knew whether she had taken the right train to North Dakota; apparently she and the train conductor used a lot of hand signs to communicate. She finally arrived at her destination: a town called Columbus, North Dakota, where some friends from Norway met her. They had helped pay for her trip and she was to work to pay them back. It was a terrible letdown for her coming to the flat state of North Dakota: poor water, no trees and gumbo all over. She worked at a hotel in town for a couple of years, where she eventually met my dad. They got married in 1909. I still remember a lot of old-timers saying, "Can't understand why a pretty girl like her didn't find a fellow sooner."

They built a small house on the flat prairies of Dakota and raised six children. Times were really rough in the early days: they had to plant a garden and spuds, raise pigs for meat, cows for cream checks, etc., and chickens for eggs and meat. We had to make do with what we had. Food was simple and plain, no fancy pies or cakes and no frills. Mother made plenty of quilts in the fall to keep us warm; it seemed as if the wind blew right through the house in those days. Straw mattresses were the thing then. Every fall my older brothers would lug the old mattresses over to the thresh pile and replace the old, ground-up straw with a new batch. Having only a three-room house left us with little sleeping room, so my youngest brother had a little box with a straw mattress that fit under the older boys' bed during the daytime and pulled out from under the bed at night. It solved the problem. My sister and I, being the youngest, always slept with our folks. It was very crowded to say the least, but always so cozy and warm. Mother always saw to it that we all had plenty of food on the table. She baked 19 loaves of bread a week; I still remember her huge wooden bread box full of good homemade bread.

As the years went by my dad finally built a living room and bedrooms onto the small house. He always hitched up his horses and hauled the cream to a nearby town once a week for groceries and supplies. He also took a load of oats to town and had the guy at the mill grind it up for cattle feed. Horses were our main source of transportation; in winter it was the sled. I remember my dad taking us to "reading for the minister" on Saturday mornings. In the summer my dad always walked to town for his leisure time and played cards with his friends at the cream station to win a few "chips." During the "dirty '30s" there was no hay for the animals, so Dad always put up Russian thistle stocks for the cattle. There were no crops in the '30s either, and people were very poor. How we survived, I'll never know. I'll never forget those Depression years and how hard they were for my mother and father. My mother and dad lived to be quite old. They finally moved off the farm to live in the town of Columbus, North Dakota, where they passed away in 1955 and 1958. Bless their hearts.

Olga Hanson
Columbus, North Dakota

Twist of Fate Determined Bloodline

Augusta Sofia Amelia Hermanson was born in Nye, Smaaland, Sweden, on April 13, 1869.

She spent much of her childhood with her maternal grand-parents, Adolph and Elizabeth Nelson, and attended a girls' school.

At age 18 or 19, she became engaged to a man named Emil. They decided Emil should go to America and save his earnings to send for her. Emil had a married brother living in Davenport, North Dakota, at the time.

In May 1890 she bade farewell to her mother, Caroline; stepfather, Carl Peterson; younger sisters, Ida and Hilda; and grandparents. After a stormy voyage, including a three day stopover in England, they arrived in New York.

Augusta took the train to Davenport, where she arrived June 5, 23 days after leaving Sweden. To her dismay she discovered Emil's brother had died, and Emil was more interested in his brother's widow. Augusta was dressed in drab, dull clothing; Emil and the widow pointed their fingers at her old-world costume and laughed. Augusta saw right away that Emil was involved with this other woman, and she was very upset. She did not have any more to do with Emil. She hired out to the Nels Braaten family, where she made many friends, especially within the Hendrick Clemenson family.

Augusta met Gilbert, who had emigrated from Norway with his parents, Hendrick and Berthe Clemenson, and family in 1870.

Augusta and Gilbert married June 6, 1891. Soon afterward they sent tickets to Augusta's sister, who later married Gilbert's brother.

Gilbert bought 160 acres from his employer, Addison Leach, and worked it until it was sold in 1894. Gilbert then rented his father's farm, purchasing it for 15,000 bushels of wheat in 1896, to be paid in yearly installments. Gilbert also served as a water-pumper for Northern Pacific Steam Engines.

Gilbert and Augusta had 12 children: Hartvig Bartinius, 1892-1903; Adolph, 1893-1974; Robert, 1895-1960; Mabel Carolina, 1897- ; Agnes Geneva, 1899-1962; Ella Randine, 1900-1906; Lillian Hazel, 1902- ; Hedvig Clementina, 1904- ; Helmer Edwin, 1910-1910; Florence Elena, 1911- ; two twins died in infancy. Augusta and Gilbert also raised Robert's two sons, Martin and Elmer, after their mother, Ella, died during the 1918 flu epidemic. Gilbert and Augusta were always ready to lend a helping hand to anyone in need. Augusta was active in the community, a skilled seamstress for family and neighbors, a Red Cross organizer during World War I and an able farm worker despite her small stature. During the war in which her son, Adolph, served, the 1918 flu epidemic struck, and Augusta kept busy caring for family and neighbors.

Augusta and Gilbert moved from the farm to Fargo, North Dakota, in 1925. Gilbert died in May of 1928.

Augusta moved to West Fargo, North Dakota, in 1948, remaining spry and active and caring for garden and house.

Augusta cared for the Clemenson family cemetery until she reached her 100th year.

She died at the Elim rest home on February 15, 1971, two months short of 102.

Augusta smoked a little white tobacco pipe and made elderberry wine. My ancestral bloodline would have been different if my grandfather had been Emil, instead of Gilbert Clemenson. That's fate.

Naomi J. Ochs.
Independence, Missouri

Homesteaders Became First Area Settlers

The family left for America on July 14, 1870, as mentioned in the Emigrate Register No. 4, folio 347. Included were: Hendrick Klemetson Greaker, 45; Berthe Arvesdtr, 38; Kristen, 16; Marta, 14; Andreas, 12; Hedvind, 7; Bernhard, 5; and Gulbrand, 2. They paid 340 daler, 60 ort in old Norwegian money—about 700 kroner today—before leaving from Tune, Norway. En route to America, the ship struck a sandbar off Ireland, where it remained for two weeks while cargo was removed to release the vessel. After five weeks at sea, they landed in the United States on August 10, 1870. They first went to Fairbault, Minnesota, on the steamboat *Hero*, for which they paid 100 daler.

The following excerpt is taken from a *Fargo Forum* article:

Living in Fairbault, Minnesota, Hendrick, who was a shoe-maker, followed his trade there. One sunny April day in 1871 he took off his leather apron, laid down his shoe-last and awl, and with his two eldest sons, Kristen and Andreas, Hendrick started west on foot to find a home.

They carried necessities in packs on their backs: two army muskets, blankets, a frying pan, salt, coffee and other needful things. They slept wherever night found them, sometimes under trees beside a lake, sometimes in a settler's stable. They shot rabbits, hen-partridges and prairie chickens and cooked them over camp-fires. The way was long, but they couldn't get lost because they didn't know where they were going.

It was a rugged trip as they frequently had to hew their way through woods and brush. Late in May, they came to where the Red River divided Fargo and Moorhead. There was a shack on the Minnesota side of the river and a log house, owned by a half-breed Indian, on the Dakota side. A Hudson Bay ferry brought the travelers across.

On they trudged, through water that practically covered the prairie. Hendrick arrived at the Sheyenne River site one and one-half miles southwest of Horace, where he put down the pack on his back. "We'll stay here," he said, after digging in the ground with a spade. "This will be fine land in a little while."

Hendrick took up squatter's rights in Section 30, Stanley township. Woods were heavy on the Sheyenne River, where they decided to settle. First they stripped off tree bark to make a crude shelter, then they began to build a log cabin. Hendrick carried many of the timber logs on his shoulders to the cabin site.

A prairie fire destroyed both those efforts, but another house was ready by late fall. Ola Holman, who had also come to settle at Horace, North Dakota, drove to Benson, Minnesota, and brought his own family and the Clemensons back in a covered wagon. Berthe and the other children joined them later that same year. There was no snow until a few days before Christmas that year, which eased their hardships. Hendrick later filed for homestead rights, becoming the first permanent settler in this area. He became the area's first postmaster, too, appointed in 1874 and serving until 1876. He was on a committee of three that named the village "Horace," in honor of Horace Greeley, who was at that time a candidate for the United States presidency. Greeley lost to Garfield, but the name Horace lived on.

With the help of his sons, Hendrick developed the prairie into a well-cultivated farm. Their children grew to adulthood at Horace. Two sons, Andrew and Gilbert, and a daughter, Mathilda, settled in the local area for their lifetime.

The first pioneers came to the Horace area in 1871-72, settling along the Sheyenne River, where there were plenty of trees for log cabins and firewood. Breaking the virgin soil with oxen and walking plow was difficult; it took a day to plow one and one-half to two acres. Occasionally, friendly Indians came up the river in canoes to ask for food or tobacco.

My mother, Lillian Clemenson Werst, grew up living with her parents and Grandmother Berthe. She spent many happy hours talking to her grandmother. My mother gave me two bread plates from the old set of family dishes that my Great-Grandmother Berthe brought on the boat with her family from Norway. These small, 120-year-old bread plates are all that remain of the set of family dishes that Berthe saved.

The Clemenson Family History Reunion is currently held every three years. From the reunions I have a complete family history book, with a computer listing of more than 3,000 relatives who are scattered over the 50 states and Canada. I have a cookbook, too: *Clemenson Cooks 120 years (1870-1990)*.

Hendrick died November 11, 1904, and Berthe at age 90 on May 8, 1921. Both are buried in the Clemenson Cemetery near the homestead in Horace, North Dakota.

Naomi J. Ochs
Independence, Missouri

Sod House Made Snug Abode

It seemed cold that early spring day in 1882 as the ship from Sweden nosed into the port of New York. The ship's rail was lined with immigrants, including a family: a father, mother, two sons and two daughters. This was Anders John Dahlgren, his wife, Mathilda, sons John Hjalmar and Carl Amil and daughters Ingrie and Carlotta Eugenia. The youngest girl, called Genie, was barely 1 year old and looked almost transparent. With their few belongings it was easy to get through customs. They had the papers and the money to get them to Chicago where Anders' sister lived.

In Chicago it was not hard to find living accommodations that were within their means, but they were not the easiest to live in. An upper-story flat was found; by walking through the door the family had moved in. There were no modern facilities, but it provided them with a roof and shelter in their new surroundings, which seemed so strange. The flat was several flights up, and all of the water had to be carried up those steps. But dirty water did not have to be carried down, for they were told to just open a window and fling it out!

Days passed before Anders got work. People did not understand his Smöland Swedish, and he knew no English. Finally a construction boss hired him to carry bricks for a building in progress. The stagings were slippery and not very solid, but it was a job to be taken gratefully. The workday lasted from dawn to dusk. The work was hard on the back and hands but Anders did not complain. The wages would pay the rent, plus food and maybe some medicine for Genie, who wasn't doing well. At mid-morning each day one of the workers was sent to a nearby saloon for a bucket of beer for the men. One worker always wanted to be sent, but he took a long time to return and drank several big swallows of beer on the way. He was not allowed to go often. The foreman noticed that Anders was truthful, honest and could be trusted, so he regularly got the beer. Once the street was muddy and Anders fell, spilling the full bucket! There was nothing to do but go back to the saloon for more beer, and this pailful had to be paid for out of his own pocket.

The boss was helpful to Anders, carefully teaching him English and showing concern, often asking him how Genie was getting along. Then the worst happened: After a few days of terrible, feverish illness it was over; Carlotta Eugenia Dahlgren was dead! The funeral, which took place in the depressing heat of August, was awful for the family.

Soon they heard that land was being given as homesteads in Dakota Territory. They saved money for the train fare and moved to land west of Athol, South Dakota. There were no buildings on the land. Friends let them dig a cavelike house in the side of a small hill. Anders was careful to shore up the roof. Buffalo grass roots gave a fuzzy look to the ceiling, which was just high enough for the parents to stand erect. A hole was made in the sod for the stovepipe, which went straight up from the stove. Four upright poles made the corners of a bed frame; a rope spring and a bag of cornhusks for the mattress were added to make it a luxurious sleeping place. The bed, a packing-box table and the stove were the only furniture. The two boys slept on quilts on the floor, and the girl slept with her parents. The mother's last chore at night was to prop the spade or the stove poker against the edges of the blanket that covered the doorway—anything to keep out the ever-present wind. Field mice joined the family in their snug abode, and it became the boys' job to catch them or drive them away. As spring came to the prairie the home was more comfortable. The mother would sprinkle water on the dirt floor when the boys scuffled and raised the dust. On June 18, 1883, another baby, Edwin Gustave, was born. City records verify that he was the first white boy born in that part of Dakota Territory. He weighed three pounds at birth. His parents did not have a scale, but the mother rigged one up with a cross-beam. Placing the baby on one side and a small pail on the other, she put lard in the pail until the beam was even. Later, when visiting folks had a scale, she weighed the pail of lard. It was three pounds.

For a short time the family moved to Farmingdale, South Dakota, where Anders raised cattle and was a horse trader, but they soon moved back to the farm near Athol. Other children born to the family were Arthur and Edith. Anders ran the farm, and at times his son, Edwin, farmed with him. Anders was also a trapper. At one time he raised skunks and sold the furs. His house was on the Nixon River, and he caught fish and turtles to feed the skunks.

When Anders was 80, he was converted during a tent meeting and joined the Calvary Wesleyan Methodist Church.

He remained active and alert until a week before his death at the age of 89 in 1937.

Eunice Hoien Dahlgren
Sweet Home, Oregon

Tried to Be a "Real American Girl"

Helga had just been through customs on Ellis Island. She picked up her shabby suitcase and took a few steps on American soil. Pausing briefly, she took a long look at her new country.

Tomorrow Helga would board a train to join her Swedish friends in Minnesota. They too had immigrated in hopes of finding a rich life in the United States.

On reaching St. Paul, Minnesota, she soon found work in a large bakery with a nicely furnished flat nearby.

Her first day at work was lonely and tiring. Darkness fell early. She noticed most of the houses had red lights in the windows. The lights looked so pretty and cheerful. "Maybe that is the custom here. If I live here I must follow their ways," she thought. A few days later she found and bought a kerosene lamp with a red glass chimney. "Now I will be a real American girl," she thought.

When the sun set, she lit her lovely new lamp and set it near the window. A short time later she heard a knock on her door. "My first visitor; it may be Elsa from next door," she thought. Instead a strange man stood on her threshold.

"How much you charge Mrs.?" he asked.

"I sell nothing, so I charge nothing." She closed the door with a bang. A short time later there came another rap on her door. Opening it cautiously, she saw her second male caller.

"What you want? Why you knock on my door?"

"I see your red light. Do you not want business?"

"Business, business, I no understand you." Again she gave the door a vicious bang.

Poor Helga. Yet a third knock came, and another gentleman stood on her stoop.

"Hullo," she greeted him.

"I say, you are a pretty one. I think I'll like you."

"I no like you. Go way, go way." Exhausted, she put out her red light and went to bed.

After a restless night, Helga was still puzzled by the deluge of male callers. She knew so few men in this new country.

"I will ask my friend Elsa," she told herself.

After an explanation from her friend, she discarded the beautiful red lamp and looked for lodging in a better neighborhood.

Helga's final thought, "I still hope I can be a real American girl."

Lillie Peters
Sioux City, Iowa

Milk Paid the Bills

My grandparents both came to America from Denmark when they were 12 years old. They crossed the ocean by ship and endured terrible hardships. They did not know each other at that time. Later they were married and lived on a farm near Tonganoxie, Kansas. They were very poor but had a cow and chickens, etc.

They had five children; my father was the youngest. When he was 2 years old, his father died of an infection caused by a hedge thorn wound. Grandmother was left alone with her children. She worked hard and raised them well. Father remembers they milked several cows, but the children were not allowed to drink more than one small cupful a day because the milk had to be sold.

Father's sisters did very well in school, getting top grades. Father did very well in sports and finally became a schoolteacher in many one-room schoolhouses.

My father, Clarence Hummelgaavd, married my mother, Audrie North, just after the Great Depression.

My father, now 82, and my mother, 85, still farm near Linwood, Kansas.

Barb Moyer
Chapman, Kansas

Gophers Paid for Clothes Trunk

John Hoien was born and raised at Øste Vraa, Denmark. When he was 19, his parents borrowed money from a banker for his ticket to America. He traveled with his sister's family, sailing from Esberg to Hull, England. There they had to wait for a ship. They slept in the station, and one night John felt hands running over his hip pockets. He rolled over and went back to sleep because he knew enough to have his money in his coat breast pocket. In the morning several people were yelling that they had been robbed!

The ship, *Saxonia*, finally came, and they embarked for Boston, arriving in May 1903. They had relatives in Iowa, so they went there first. Then John heard that there was work to be had in South Dakota. He went to Conde, where he got a job as a section hand on the railroad between Conde and Groton.

As he worked, he noticed a lot of gophers along the right-of-way. John secured some traps and set them as the crew went out in the morning. He collected the gophers as the crew came home at night. He was paid 2 cents a tail for the gophers. It was not long before he had enough money to buy a trunk in which to keep his clothes, all paid for by the gophers.

John did not have boots or work shoes and was struggling to make his thin-soled shoes hold together until he got his first pay. With this money he went to a dry-goods store in Conde run by Mr. Place, where he was fitted with a good pair of work shoes. There John had his first experience with a merchant offering to "put it on the cuff" if the customer had no money. But John had money and paid for the shoes. To show his pleasure, Mr. Place threw in a pair of work socks to boot.

John worked on the section and also for farmers. He spent almost no money on himself, so in two years he had sent enough money to his parents to pay off their loan.

Eunice Hoien Dahlgren
Sweet Home, Oregon

Ailing Child Narrowly Survived Journey

My Grandfather Swen was born in Sogne, Norway, in 1840. At 18 he came to America; at 21 he purchased a farm in southern Minnesota. His parents, with their remaining seven children, embarked on a sailing vessel in 1861, headed for America. After a long and hazardous voyage of two and one-half months, they landed at Quebec. They carried their provisions for the journey. The youngest child waxed exceeding ill and at one time was thought to be dead, but thankfully he lived, as a burial at sea would have been heartbreaking. They first went to Iowa and later homesteaded in southern Minnesota near Swen. My grandmother, Sarah, came with her parents and family from East Toten, Norway, landing in New York in 1853. They were among the first permanent settlers in Mower County. Swen and Sarah were married in 1861 and had 13 children, nine of whom lived to adulthood. Two of Sarah's sisters married two of Swen's brothers. Today Swen and Sarah have nine living grandchildren. The two oldest are 86—about the same age Sarah was at her death.

My maternal great-grandparents came from England and Bohemia. William Withers married Sarah Smith in 1820. She died in 1842, leaving eight children. William remarried, and his second wife and the children left Bentworth, England, in 1844. They landed in America about two months later and went to Westfield, New York. William and Martha had six children; Grandfather Warren was the third one. He was born in 1848 and lived until 1938—and was the last one living. Franz Novotny, a weaver, married Theresa Houdek in Bohemia. They came to America for religious freedom. They settled in Wisconsin. They had six children. My Grandmother Cecelia married Warren Withers in 1873, and they had six children. Three grandchildren remain from this marriage.

Erma Hawkins
Tucson, Arizona

Grandpa Reached Destination Four Years Later

When my grandfather left Norway in 1870 at age 21, he had in his possession a Certificate of Removal, signed by the Minister of Nerstrand, Norway. It stated his name, date of birth, his parents' names and that "In occasion of his removal to America, I confirm that he has not bound a friend with public promise of marriage, and I do not know anything disadvantageous about the way he has behaved." He boarded a sailboat, which if the winds were favorable, could cross the ocean in five weeks. Unfortunately, this ship encountered many bad storms along the way, and the westerly winds caused them to drift backward many a day. The journey lasted longer than the provisions on board. In time, the food came to an end. Days passed with no land sightings, and the passengers grew desperate. Finally it was decided that they would cast lots to see who would have to sacrifice his life to feed the others. After the lots were drawn, it was customary to wait three days before taking action. Fortunately, land was sighted on the third day!

A group of travel-weary, grateful Norwegians disembarked at Quebec, Canada, after 14 weeks aboard their sailing vessel. Hungry, lonely and unable to understand the strange language, my grandfather set out to find work. He was grateful to secure a position loading wheat on steamboats. With a large bag balanced on each shoulder, he cautiously walked the narrow plank from the land to the boat, knowing that one misstep would throw him in the water.

His destination was Iowa, where friends and relatives had settled. After a few weeks he moved on to Wisconsin, where he found employment in a sawmill. Later he journeyed to Rushford, Minnesota, and worked on the railroad. For a year and a half, he labored long hours and drew only as much of his wages as he needed to live on. When he was certain he had enough money to make it to Iowa, he went to collect his accumulation of wages, only to find that the section boss had skipped out, taking the entire payroll with him.

Discouraged, my grandfather hopped aboard a freight train

and got a free ride to Hayfield, Minnesota, where he found work on a farm. When haying time came, they pitched the hay onto a flat rack pulled by a team of horses. Grandfather stood atop the load to stack the hay. The rack rocked back and forth, moving across the rough slough, and since there was nothing to hang onto, Grandfather was thrown from the load and run over by the wheels of the rack. Both of his legs were broken. No doctor was available, so he tied boards on each of his legs and laid with these splints until his bones healed.

After recovering, he moved to New Sharon, Iowa, where he finally reached his relatives. It was now 1873. Folks worked long hours to earn 50 cents a day. The Panic of 1873 had forced the banks to close, and many merchants had to accept eggs and butter as payment for merchandise. Grandfather labored in this area until he had enough money to purchase a wagon and a team of horses.

With his prized possessions, he drove to Hamilton County, Iowa, where he arrived at the home of a good friend from Norway. After four years, he had finally reached his destination! Land adjoining his friend's farm was for sale, so Grandfather purchased 80 acres for $7.50 an acre. He paid $100 down and got a mortgage for $500 at 15 percent interest. Four years later he had to increase that mortgage to $530. That fall he had a good corn crop, so he fattened up his 60 head of hogs and chased them to the nearest railway station, 20 miles away, where he received 2 cents a pound for each hog. That kept him from losing the farm.

There were many struggles ahead, but with his strong body, tireless energy, tenacious courage and strong faith in God, he became a successful pioneer who lived within his means and cared for his obligations, taught himself English by reading the Bible, married, reared nine children and was proud to be an American.

Jeanette Larson
Story City, Iowa

Mother Made Extra-Sticky Pancakes

In 1909 my mother first set foot on Ellis Island, the entrance to "The Promised Land." She had grown up on Stjerne Island in Norway and had an eighth-grade education but no English. My father came over the same year from Skäne, Sweden. He likewise knew no English. They met at a Scandinavian Club and married in 1915. In the years that followed, they taught themselves to read, write, and speak English very well. It wasn't always easy!

Pursuing Dad's dream of owning land "like Skäne," they migrated to Iowa, where their first jobs were hired man/housekeeper for two Swedish bachelors. The bachelors worked hard and demanded good, solid food—food that would "stick to their ribs." They wanted pancakes for every breakfast.

One morning when Mother started her pancakes, she discovered that she was out of flour. Since she was miles from the store, she was at a loss for what to do, until she remembered there was a sack of flour in the storeroom. She hurriedly scooped up two cups and proceeded to make breakfast. Mother was famous for her good pancakes, but alas, these were terrible! The bachelors took one bite and wondered what had happened. When mother explained about the flour, they went to the storeroom. There was the sack, plainly marked "wallpaper paste!" She had recognized the "past" in paste and thought it related to "pastry"; hence, it must be flour. They teased her about her pancakes for years. One thing about them—I'll bet they stuck to their ribs.

Through hard work and thriftiness my parent's attained my dad's dream of owning land. They are gone now, but I still own a piece of that dream in Iowa. I hope to hand it down to my children so that the dream will go on.

Helen B. Baker
Lexington, Missouri

Timing Saved Family from *Titanic* Voyage

Grandpa Stromsoe had already traveled to America seeking better work prospects. He left Grandma and two children behind in Sweden. He sent for his family after saving enough money for the passageway on the ship *Titanic*. When Grandma got the travel money, she made ready to leave Sweden and go to England to catch the great new "unsinkable ship." The children were excited about this trip to a faraway land across the ocean. They journeyed from the northern part of Sweden by train, then caught a boat to England. Fortunately, they missed their connection with the *Titantic*. There was nothing to do but transfer the tickets to the *Lusitania* and come on to Ellis Island in America. The ship took almost three weeks to cross the Atlantic in 1912. After being shuttled through the medical checks at Ellis Island, they boarded the train for Denver, Colorado. After settling in Denver, Grandma declared that since they were in America now they would only speak English. Grandma taught herself to read and write by studying the dictionary.

The two children were soon joined by another baby. Suddenly Grandma began to be terribly homesick for the old country.

My mother was their second child, who crossed the ocean three times to finally settle in America. She is no longer living, and I regret not asking more specific questions about those times.

Shirley Vogl
Fort Lupton, Colorado

Everything Was Good but the Gooseberry Pie

My grandmother was only 16 when she and two young men left Norway in 1893 and sailed to America. Their boat landed in New York, where they boarded a train to Ames, Iowa. The uncomfortable benches made the trip seem endless as they rode for several days to reach Iowa. Three cold, hungry and lonesome young people stepped off the train at 9 p.m. into the chilly April night. It was a long wait until 3 a.m., when they boarded another train to travel 15 miles north to Randall, Iowa. Since they were scheduled to arrive the night before, there was no welcoming party to meet them at 5 a.m. Too excited to wait, they left their luggage and started walking. It was cold and rainy and there were traces of snow in the ditches. As Grandma trudged through the sticky black mud, her low shoes growing colder and heavier, she wondered just where her brother's farm was located. Her first impression of America was anything but the land of riches and wealth that had been described to her.

After walking five miles, they arrived at her brother's home. They stopped at the straw stack and wiped off their muddy shoes before going to the house, where they received a warm welcome. They feasted on warm pancakes while they reported on the folks back home and gave an account of their long journey.

That summer Grandma lived with her sister and family, and on November 2 she married a brother of her sister's husband, who had paid her fare to America. A seamstress came to the house and stayed for several days to sew the long, white wedding dress. Bakers also came to the home to bake and cook plenty of food for the many people who came to the wedding and stayed all day. It was a joyous occasion. The food was delicious, except for the gooseberry pie, which was so sour most of it went in the swill bucket.

At the age of 16, Grandma was a farm wife in Iowa. Babies came along every two years until there were 14. One baby died, and the older children had left home when the youngest were born, but there were always children to care for and work to do. They reared their large family on 80 acres of land. They were never wealthy, but they had a happy Christian home where everyone learned to work and become good citizens. They left us a great heritage.

Jeanette Larson
Story City, Iowa

Pioneer "Sells" Family on America

My uncle, C.J. Burdette, came to Creston from Sweden as a young man. He left Sweden because he had older brothers and property was left to the oldest son. He married Christina Danielson of another pioneer family. Her brothers were stalwart men who were homesteaders and railroaders.

People from Sweden usually went to Minnesota or the Fairfield, Iowa, area. Uncle Charley went to Fairfield. In Sweden his name was Anderson. There were so many Andersons in that area that he decided to take the name Burdette, a German name. They admired German people.

He soon made enough money to make a trip "home," where he sold America to his younger brother as well as his sister, who became my mother. A younger brother and a cousin east of Creston welcomed them here.

Some of the men were railroaders, so some settled in Creston. Some went on to Denver and eventually to the West Coast.

One of the first who came over made enough money to send for his family. Their children all died with scarlet fever the first year. The mother came west and had another family of stalwart men and one daughter, who became my aunt. She too had a family in Creston.

I stayed with them one year to attend high school, then went to a new consolidated school.

I am 84 years old. I taught school for nine years, married and had four children. My son is buying my farm now.

Mildred B. Busch
Winterset, Iowa

Family Proud of Homeland and American Heritage

On May 5, 1909, my mother disembarked from an ocean liner onto Ellis Island. Everyone was glad to leave the ship. Third class, or "steerage," was very crowded, and many were seasick coming across. Mother was 17 years old—a typical Norwegian girl. She wore her Sunday clothes: a white, long-sleeved "waist" and a black wool skirt long enough to cover her high-top shoes. When let down, her brown hair was long enough for her to sit on, but it was neatly braided and pinned up under her hat.

She wasn't long on Ellis Island, for she had a cousin to meet and a job already waiting. She worked as both an upstairs maid and a cook for wealthy New Yorkers, until she and my father were married. When Pop was courting Mom, she worked for the Putnam family. Their son, George, a small boy at the time, made a nuisance of himself whenever Pop came to call. George Putnam later married Amelia Earhardt and promoted her flying career. (This was Mom's only claim to fame!)

My father came from southern Sweden on November 17, 1909, also at the age of 17. He came through Ellis Island, and he, too, had family here and a job waiting. Although he had grown up on a farm, he was a blacksmith by trade, and one of his first jobs was fitting door handles on Packard cars. He met my mother at a Scandinavian club, and after a trip to Sweden and Norway to meet their families, they were married April 3, 1915. His wedding suit cost $3.50. They eventually settled in Iowa and raised four children. When we were young, we children were often embarrassed by their accents and old-country ways.

Father had borrowed money for passage to America. His first job paid $3 for 60 or more hours of work. He not only paid off the loan quickly, he was able to retire when he was 53 years old!

They both had eight years of school in the old country, but it did not include English, and the math was all metric system. They learned both in a hurry over here so no one could cheat them. Pop was the most honest man I ever knew.

The greatest legacy they gave me was their inherent love of music. They both sang a lot, and my father played the accordion. He loved to dance and taught Mom. She didn't know how because she was raised on a tiny island where their activities were all at church. Times were hard in the '30s, but somehow they scraped up $100 to buy a piano for me, the only girl, so I could take lessons. They would be so proud if they knew that I play the organ at church.

When I was 6, Mother took me home to Norway with her. I remember that it was beautiful, but still rather primitive—no electricity or plumbing, not even a bridge from the mainland. We went by boat. I met my only grandparent, Mom's father, but all I can remember of him was his red hair and red beard, and that he loved to chew on coffee beans! He died a year before the Nazis invaded Norway. One of Mom's sisters and her only brother also came to America. Her brother was killed in an explosion aboard the ship he worked on; her sister died in childbirth.

Of my father's seven siblings, only three came to America. When their father died, the land and money was left to the boys, European style. Pop had to go back to Sweden to collect his share. After they came to America, my folks saw the advent of automobiles, radios, movies, television, airplanes—even a man on the moon! They loved America, but never lost their love for their homelands. I'm glad they came, and I am very proud of my heritage.

Bernice Johnson Baker
Lexington, Missouri

Ancestor Volunteered for Civil War Service

I was born on the farm of Østerud in Hurdal on February 22, 1831, baptized on March 13, 1831, and confirmed October 21, 1846. I journeyed to America on April 5, 1854. Thus began the story of Gulbrand Hanson Østerud, later known as Gilbert Hanson, the second son of Hans Gulbrandson Østerud and Kari Gulliksdatter and the first of the Hanson clan to migrate to America.

During his first two years in America, 1854-56, Gulbrand lived in Racine County, Wisconsin. He and Ole Oleson Østerud worked together on a farm near Yorkville. It is likely that he went to Green Bay to work in the pineries, chopping timber in the winter months. He is not mentioned by name in the letter of November 20, 1854, which was written by Hans Christian Gullickson, but Ole and Gullickson were to leave for Green Bay on November 24 and would stay there until the first of April. Pay for working in the pineries was $25 per month plus room and board.

In the summer of 1854 there was a cholera epidemic. Many of the newcomers died. The people blamed the American food and the hot weather for the disease, but the swampy Muskego area and the poor sanitation were probably the real reasons for the epidemic. The miserable sickness led to 10 or 12 burials per day. With the coming of cold weather the epidemic slackened, but the summers of 1855-56 were apparently just as bad.

In September 1856 Gulbrand and Ole set out for Minnesota. Ole wrote: "Muskego is the worst pest-hole I have ever been in ..." and they moved to "the healthy place."

They left Racine, Wisconsin, passing through Beloit, Wisconsin; Dunleith (now East Dubuque), Illinois; Lansing, Waukon, Freeport, Decorah and Ridgeway, Iowa, according to Ole's diary. The route suggests that they took the train from Racine to East Dubuque (a railroad follows this route on an 1854 map of Wisconsin) and a boat up the Mississippi River to Lansing. From Lansing they went inland in Iowa to Ridgeway where, the story goes, they met their friends, the Hallings, Hellicksons and Olsons, all of whom traveled together to Minnesota.

Nearing Spring Valley, they stopped at the John Bateman farm and inquired about land with woods and water. Mr. Bateman told them to go southwest about three miles, where they would find good land. They went, one mile east and one-half mile south from Ostrander. Gulbrand and Ole took for themselves adjoining 100-acre farms in Section 33. According to an act of Congress approved March 3, 1855, the land was military bounty, but the man to whom it was originally assigned didn't want it, so it was available for settlement. The two men arrived on their farms October 8, 1856. Gulbrand had his worldly goods shipped from Racine, at a cost of $11.25. On October 16 they went to Chatfield to register their land at the General Land Office. Gulbrand's land was patented on April 10, 1860, by President James Buchanan.

It is a fine piece of land, one of the best in the area: high and gently rolling. The south branch of the Root River flows a short distance north of this farm. The soil is glacial drift loam. Originally the farm had a great deal of timber, which was a source of firewood and building materials. The woodland ran from its present location, next to the house, to the cemetery.

Nothing is known of Gulbrand's first years on the farm except that he had to go to Decorah for supplies and to have his grain ground. Arriving in October, he must have had to build a shelter to live in that first winter. The settlers didn't waste time getting their land under the plow and growing crops such as wheat, barley, rye and corn. They also raised hogs for meat. Later, as they were able to acquire them, they raised cattle and poultry and planted fruit trees.

The first house Gulbrand built on his land was a solid structure that is still standing today. It is a double-walled house, built of upright log studs covered inside and out with broad sawed boards. The spaces between the two walls were filled with sawdust. Later, the outside of the house was covered with clapboard. It is a two-story house, containing two rooms: one downstairs and one up.

A number of the early settlers in the area came from Hurdal, Norway. They founded a little village named Hurdal, which was located at the first crossroads north of the farm. It had a store, two blacksmith shops and a few houses. The village has disappeared, and the corner is now a pasture.

Their post office, which opened in the spring of 1856, was in the village of Etna, two miles east of the homestead, near the Root River.

Gulbrand's brothers, Lars Norgaarden and Andreas (Andrew) Hanson, with their wives and children, came to America in 1857 and settled on farms nearby. There were still Indians in Minnesota at that time and Andrea's wife, Maria, had a scare one day when she came into the house from the field and found one standing in the kitchen. He said he wanted some food, which she gave him, and he went on his way.

In 1861 Gulbrand's father, Hans Gulbrandson Østerud, came to America in the company of his daughter Caroline, "Lena," his oldest daughter, Ingeborg, and Ingeborg's husband and four children. Hans' wife, Kari Gullicksdatter Østerud, had died in November 1858. His sons were in this country, and there had been crop failures in Norway, so, 66 years old and blind, Hans came to spend his remaining years here.

Their party arrived by boat at McGregor, Iowa. Hans' son, Lars Norgaarden, met them with a wagon and team of oxen. All the baggage was piled on the wagon and Hans and some of the others rode on top. Caroline, Lars and the rest of the travelers walked the 125 miles to Bloomfield.

The Civil War had broken out, and on November 6, 1862, Gulbrand was sworn in as a First Regiment private in the Minnesota Mounted Rangers; he had volunteered to serve for 12 months in the United States Army. He enlisted under the name of Gilbert Hanson, which is the first known record of him changing his name. He was mustered in at Ft. Snelling, Minnesota. Roll-call vouchers do not show where he served in the army until the summer of 1863, when it was noted that he was absent from roll call because of being "on detached service as escort to a provision train to Locquin Partes." It has been said that he guarded prisoners of war on a troop train. He was mustered out on December 1, 1863. Gilbert's brother, Andreas

"Andrew," was drafted into the army at this time. Their father and Andrew's wife took care of their farms for them while they were gone. On August 24, 1864, Gilbert voluntarily re-enlisted, this time into Company I of the 11th Regiment of Minnesota Volunteers. He was mustered into the service at Ft. Snelling on September 1, 1864, for a period of one year. He was paid a bounty of $100 for this enlistment and $53.12 for clothing. He was mustered out of the army on June 26, 1865, at Gallatin, Tennessee.

Dorothy Collins
San Antonio, Texas

Iowa Suited Norwegian Settlers

Crowded conditions, poverty and rigid discipline induced many of the people in Norway to come to the United States. It meant that they had to save what they could in order to book passage to the New World and buy enough food to get them through the arduous trip. It was a sad occasion leaving family members behind whom they probably would never see again.

They took whatever clothing they could on the trip, hoping it would last until they could find work. They faced unknown dangers in the New World.

Once they landed, arrangements were made for them to travel westward. They rode trains, got boat rides on big rivers and the Great Lakes and worked across country. They also encountered people who cheated them.

By the 1840s, the Norwegian immigrants were arriving in Wisconsin. Many came to Rock Prairie, where they had relatives, but they found that the government ground had already been taken, which left Iowa as a likely spot.

Those who came to Allamakee County did so accidentally. In October 1849, Ole Larson, Ole O. Storla, Svend Hesla and Nels Roe left their relatives in Rock County and began their long walk to find a spot. They originally intended to visit the area south of the Turkey River settlement in Clayton County. As they traveled across the Mississippi River, the operator of the ferry between Prairie du Chien and McGregor advised them to go to Allamakee County.

After landing where Paint Creek emptied into the Mississippi River, they were advised to go westward on an Indian trail along the creek. They followed the creek to a place the Indians called Big Springs. This was the site of Waukon, the county seat. They hesitated and went back to spots where markets were being built.

Fewer than nine miles from the Mississippi River, Hesla found a sparkling spring; this looked to him like a logical place to homestead. It happened to be the center of Paint Creek Township. One-half mile southeast, Hesla found another spring for Erick Kittelson, a friend who hadn't come with them.

Two miles north, another spring was found to satisfy Ole O. Storla. Roe and Larson wanted to be closer to the Mississippi River, so they settled in Taylor Township.

These men were accustomed to the hilly areas of Norway.

They returned to Wisconsin and pointed out the advantages of their finds. On May 8, 1850, eight settlers and their families set out from Rock Prairie to Paint Creek, driving their cattle and hogs ahead of them. They crossed the Mississippi River on a ferry operated by a horse. They went westward along the Yellow River until they found a natural bridge at Monona.

The distance was about 130 miles, and it took 21 days to cover. After the third group arrived and felt they were there to stay, they organized a church and school. The church is still in operation, but the school was closed and removed. A consolidated school was built in 1922-23.

Crude, primitive shelters and wagons served as parlor, kitchen and dormitories. Shelters were composed of crutches from trees, with poles laid on the ends. They used elm ends and bark to keep the rains out. There were no doors.

One man converted a hollow basswood tree, stuffed it with hay and crawled inside. He used a knothole for ventilation.

Soon log houses were built and roofed with birch bark and turf.

Food was simple, but plentiful. Coffee and brown sugar had to be bought. Salt pork, salt beef and other meat was made into dried beef and sausage. They made bread from their own wheat, corn meal cake, mush, lefse and later, sorghum.

Water came from springs, and sheep wool was woven into yarn. This would be knit into clothing.

Cattle grazed. Prairie grass was as high as a man. They made rail fences; it took 4,480 rails and 1,500 stakes to fence 40 acres. This represented a lot of work. Some fences were also built of smooth rocks. These were permanent.

Wolves, foxes and wildcats—plus a few skunks—were plentiful; strychnine exterminated them. Prairie hens, quail and pheasants provided a variety of meat. The streams had plenty of fish.

Oxen were used for transportation and field work.

Grain was seeded by hand. Later a three-shovel cultivator was bought. Harrows were made by using two logs, fastened at one end with iron pegs about 10 inches apart. Hay was cut with a scythe. Grain bundles were tied by hand.

As time went on the families prospered. They built log houses, which were sided and later enlarged. They were hard-working religious people. Many of their descendants still live in northeast Iowa.

Madonna Storla
Postville, Iowa.

A Satisfying Life in the Promised Land

Times were hard in Norway. Down through the generations the farms had been divided and subdivided. A son of the family may have gone higher up on the mountain, cut down some trees, built a house, cleared a little plot of land and eked out a living. But that could not go on forever. The oldest son inherited the farm. His siblings had to go out to work for others. By the 1830s there was little work to be had and wages were very low. Because of restrictive laws they could not change their occupations. The children had very little education. They read well enough to read the Bible and be confirmed. Some boys were taught writing and arithmetic. The girls did not learn those things because women had no need for them. In Norway, when people moved from farm to farm they changed their name to the name of the farm. Some people had several names in their lifetime.

In 1838 a pamphlet, "True Account of America," was published in Christiania (Oslo). It was written in America by Ole Rynning and described the country in such glowing terms that many got "America fever." They sold their possessions and scraped together enough money to go to the wonderful Land of Opportunity.

The usual route was by sailboat to New York, by steamer up the Hudson River to Albany, by canal boat to Buffalo and by steamer on the Great Lakes to Milwaukee or Chicago. From New York to Buffalo it cost from $3 to $4 and from Buffalo to Chicago, $9 to $12. Children from 2 to 12 went for half price, and infants were free. Freight wagons to their destination usually cost about $1 per 100 pounds. Another immigrant route, by way of New Orleans, went up the Mississippi and Ohio Rivers and by canal boat to Chicago. Later, some came by way of Quebec.

Ole Aslesen was born in 1813 on the Myran farm in Sigdal, Norway. This farm was on fairly level land at the upper end of Lake Soneran, along the banks of the river that fed the lake. When Ole was 3 years old his father, Asle, drowned. His mother, Kari, remarried. Her new husband, Nils, moved to her farm and, as was the custom, took the Myran name. Kari had three more children. When Ole was 16 years old his stepfather died. After his military obligation was taken care of, Ole bought the farm. He was 23 years old.

Ole got America fever and sold the farm. On May 17, 1840, at the age of 27, he left Drammen on the *Emily,* a creaky old sailing ship. The captain had said that the bottom of the ship was 150 years old. During a bad storm the timbers that supported the upper berths gave way, dropping the upper berths down on the lower ones. The passage from Drammen to New York cost 33 Norwegian speciedalers for adults and 25 speciedalers for children. Meals cost 12 speciedalers.

Ole settled in southern Wisconsin. He wrote a letter home advising his family to come to America. The next year, 50-year-old Kari Myran and her youngest son, 15-year-old Helge Nilsen Myran, set sail for America.

Ole's other half-brother, Asle Nilsen Myran, came to Wisconsin in 1843. He worked in the lead mines for a while. He returned to Norway and was married there.

Before the arrival of a minister, the settlers held lay services in a barn. Ole donated logs and helped to build the Muskego Church. He was a member of the church board. The church was dedicated in 1845. It was the first Norwegian Lutheran church in America. This building has been moved to the grounds of the Lutheran Theological Seminary in St. Paul, Minnesota.

Ole Myran used the name Ole M. Aslesen when he first came to America. He was among the signers of a document called "An American Manifesto," also called "The Muskego Manifesto." It was written in response to articles that were published in Norwegian newspapers trying to discourage emigration. The following is a partial quote: "We have no expectation of gaining riches. But we live under a liberal government in a fruitful land, where freedom and equality are the rule in religious as in civil matters, and where each one of us is at liberty to earn his living practically as he chooses ... We have no reason to regret the decision that brought us to this country."

But this new land was not the land of milk and honey that they had been promised. For many it was the land of death and despair.

In 1848 cholera appeared at the same time in New York and New Orleans, carried on two shiploads of immigrants from a cholera-infested region in Germany. They spread the disease along both immigrant routes. In 1849 Norwegian immigrants contracted the disease and brought it to the settlements in southern Wisconsin. The established settlers had to make room for the newcomers in their tiny log cabins, sod huts and dugouts. They knew nothing about sanitation or how diseases were spread. The sick and well occupied the same beds and ate from the same spoons and dishes.

A hospital was established in a large barn by Big Muskego Lake, where many people died. Graves were dug, ready for the next burial.

The settlers also suffered with malaria, dysentery, typhoid fever and "summer complaint." In Norway they had pure water which they took from the brooks running down from the snow-capped mountains. In America they hauled water from springs and stored it in barrels. Soon the water would be covered in green scum and mosquito pupae. They strained it through a cloth before they drank it. If they didn't have a spring, they dug a shallow hole near a standing pool and dipped up the water that seeped in. Their wells were so shallow that they became contaminated by surface water. They had no outhouses. The swill pail was used as a chamber pot. The pails were dumped on the ground, where the chickens scratched, the hogs rooted and the flies swarmed. They had no refrigeration. Their food sat on open shelves.

During the cholera epidemic of 1849, Ole tended the sick, made coffins and helped bury the dead. Those who became sick usually died within six hours. Every day he wondered if he would be alive the following morning. We do not know if Ole's house and living conditions were more sanitary than the average, but neither he nor Kari or Helge caught the disease.

Ole married Turi, a widow with three children, whose husband had died of cholera just after they arrived in America in 1849. Her husband, Petter Blekeberg, had been Ole's neighbor in Norway.

By now, Iowa Territory had been opened for settlement. Ole went on foot to look for better land. He pitched his tent on a high hill about eight miles west of Decorah, Iowa. He chose land in the valley to the north of the hill. In 1851 he paid $50 for 40 acres of land. He built a log cabin and brought his new family to their new home. At the time he settled there he knew of no other white man to the west of his farm.

After Ole had cut down trees to build his cabin, he planted corn between the stumps. To plant corn in sod, he used an ax to cut a gash. Then he dropped 3 or 4 kernels into the slit. When he had managed to break ground with a plow, he used a hoe to plant his corn. He marked an x with the hoe, dropped the corn in, covered it and tamped it down. The corn was carried in a bag strapped to the planter's chest. For faster germination the corn was soaked overnight.

Several times Ole and his family were frightened by Indians. One time they heard of a band of Indians coming their way and fled, leaving the farm in the charge of a hired man. He was willing to stay and take care of the stock because he had found a good hiding place. The massacring Indians had been turned back in Minnesota, so the family returned to the farm.

Turi had a son, Asle, in 1852. In 1854 she died of childbed fever. Her baby daughter was buried in her arms. Ole was left with three stepchildren and a 2-year-old son. In 1856 he married Ingri Skare. She had come from Eggedal, Norway, in 1852, along with her sister, Mari. Ole and Ingri had six children.

During the Civil War, Ole's stepson enlisted in the Norwegian Regiment, the Wisconsin 15th Infantry, on January 25, 1862. He used the name Sever Pederson. He was 15 years and 4 months old. Other young men left at the same time. As they walked down the road they shouted "Hurrah" with their caps, as a family member later related. On his 16th birthday, Sever was on a forced march somewhere between Nashville and Louisville. The Battle of Stone

River started on December 30, 1862. The next day the regiment was almost surrounded. The troops scattered and the Rebel cavalry took many captives. A Rebel cavalryman ordered Sever to surrender. When he saw Union cavalrymen coming out of the woods, he killed the Rebel, saving himself and many of his comrades. On January 2, 1863, they drove the Rebels back two miles. They had no tents, fires or food, and it was raining. They were knee-deep in mud and soaked to the skin. On his 17th birthday Sever was crossing Lookout Mountain. Seven days later, on September 20, 1863, he was taken prisoner at the Battle of Chickamauga.

He was taken to Andersonville Prison, where he died of exposure and starvation on September 5, 1864, eight days before his 18th birthday. He was buried in grave number 7,893. He was posthumously given the rank of Brevet Captain because of his bravery during the Stone River Battle.

Ole became a United States citizen on July 11, 1852. After he had lived in Iowa a few years he used the name Ole A. Myran. He gradually broke ground and increased the size of his fields. He bought more land and sold some of it later. He had good crops and bad; he was in debt now and then. He may not always have had milk and honey, but I think he was satisfied with his life in the Promised Land. He died in 1894 at the age of 81.

This man was my great-grandfather.

Rosella Goettelman
Decorah, Iowa

Chapter Three: Germanic Forebears

Great-Grandmother Greased the Tracks

In the mid 1800s, my great-grandmother, Helena Halmos, came to America from Prussia. She married Christoff Meyer, from Trier, Germany, and settled near Weeping Water, Nebraska. The railroad ran through the field just behind their stone house. (The old stone house is still standing, and the railroad tracks still run back of the house). There was an incline behind the house. The train repeatedly ran over her ducks and geese. My great-grandmother greased the tracks with hog lard to make the train slow down and give her geese a chance to get off the tracks. After a couple times when they could not make it up the little hill until they got out and wiped the tracks clean, they knocked on her back door and asked how much they owed her for her geese and ducks. They paid her, and she quit greasing the tracks.

> Melba Meyer Wiggins
> Paden, Oklahoma

Family Tree Has Widespread Branches

When my great-great-grandparents, Joseph Leis and Agatha Hoover, left Bavaria with their four children, Peter, 15; Agatha, 12; Adam, 8; and Paul, 4, there was no Statute of Liberty or welcoming committee to greet them when they arrived in New York Harbor on June 29, 1844.

I try to imagine how they felt when they left their family and homeland, with its green countryside and beautiful Bavarian Alps. Napoleon had already left his mark on their country, proclaiming Maximilian I Joseph first absolute monarch of Bavaria.

In America, immigration was the human energy that would fuel the farms and factories of a growing nation. Immigrants were the cheap labor for the factories and new farms that were blooming on the prairies of the Midwest. The family settled in Bismarck, Huron County, Ohio. Today the town is known as St. Sebastian.

Ten years after their arrival, Peter Leis married Margrate Irish, who arrived in America from Prussia. Their marriage took place in St. Sebastian Catholic Church in Bismarck, Ohio, on June 10, 1854. To this marriage 14 children were born; six in Bismarck, and eight in Bellevue, Ohio. John, their eldest son, was my grandfather. John married Emilie Jung. The Jung family came to America via Canada. After coming to the United States, the Jung family changed their name to Young, the English version of Jung.

The Leis family that arrived 150 years ago is only one branch of our family tree. In graveyards across the country my ancestors sleep. Joseph Leis is buried in St. Sebastian Cemetery (Bismarck) Ohio. His tombstone says:

Joseph Leis
Joseph, Son of Mike and Margareta (Bullion) Leis
Born: 1787 Bavaria, Germany
Got in New York June 29, 1844
Died: In Sherman TWP, Ohio, 1869 August 13
"Here you have your rest, tired out in the cold grave, the Creator was not disappointed who gave you this earthly life."

The inscription is in German.

Olivia M. Roth
Silver Spring, Maryland

Thrift Paid Off

My father's future in his home country was not very bright. He had an older brother who would get the "home place." After working on a river in Germany for five years he decided to leave home and find opportunity in America. In 1927 my father came to America to be a hired man for a farmer at Tilden, Nebraska. The farmer, whose sister lived in my father's neighborhood, had asked for two men from the community to come and work for him. There were two tickets to get them to America. My father took the chance at the age of 23. He worked for the farmer to pay off his trip on the ship. Then he worked for various other farmers.

After working for three years he wrote to ask the girl he left behind to come and marry him, and they would start farming on their own rented farm. The remaining ticket was used for her to come. They were married on April 11, 1930, and started farming.

The following March their first daughter was born. This was in the '30s, when times were probably as hard as they ever were, with low prices and drought doing battle against the farmer.

A little more than a year later a second daughter was born; that was me. After four more daughters they had a son.

My parents were thrifty, as most people were at the time. Their friends were couples who had come from their neighborhood in Germany. Some had attended the same school or lived nearby. We had parties together and a picnic every summer with these Germans.

Both of my parents worked very hard. My mother passed away at the age of 57. My father lived until he was 87.

When he entered the nursing home he was to give a story of his life. He said he came to America to make a fortune for himself. He did indeed. He owned 600 acres debt free and had CDs in the bank.

He had six daughters and a son, all of whom married. Together they gave him a total of 22 grandchildren.

Olga Feyerherm
West Point, Nebraska

Immigrant Searched for Better Life

In 1844, my great-great-grandfather, Charles Barlett Pflum, came from Germany to the New York port of entry. The port of embarkation was Le Havre, France. Records are in the St. Louis Public Library. Ship records are there also.

Charles was 18 when he chose to leave his trouble-torn birth country. He was listed as a mechanic and blacksmith on the ship's record, and he worked for his passage on the ship. He brought with him a brother named John.

In New York City, the two brothers became separated and were never reunited.

My great-great-grandfather found various jobs and worked his way to the city of St. Louis, Missouri. There he found work as a cooper, making barrels for the breweries in the beer-making city.

He eventually became so fond of America that he felt compelled to return to his homeland to bring more of his relatives to the freedom and good life he found in this good land. His father and sister returned with him to make their home in St. Louis. In the course of time his father died. The sister, the brother and his city-born wife decided they wanted to leave the city and return to the country life from which they had come in the old country. They were farm people at heart.

They settled in northeast Missouri on a rural farm. It was a small farm of 40 acres. The family was listed on the United States Census in 1861 in Shelby County Communal Colony, Bethel, Missouri. The village of Bethel was noted at that time for its distillery. Corn whiskey was a product, thus, there was a need for the cooper and the barrels he made. Great-Great-Grandfather's occupation was listed as cooper or barrel maker and farmer.

Bethel, Missouri, is a place of interest today. It was the most successful and long-lasting communal colony in Missouri, and one of the most successful in the nation. It is now registered with the

Missouri and National Historical Societies as a national historic site. The annual Bethel, Shelby County, Missouri, Harvest Fest held in October attracts visitors from all over the United States.

My great-grandfather was a working member of that colony and so accepted on the census record in the year of 1861.

At the time of the Civil War, my great-great-grandfather was living on his 40-acre farm with his wife and nine children. He surely must have been adding to his family income by also working as a cooper and barrel maker in the village of Bethel.

He did not participate in the Civil War. Perhaps he thought his first duty lay at home with his nine children and bedfast expectant wife. He was captured and taken to Palmyra, Missouri, to "join up" or "help participate." He escaped his captors, and, being a small man, he hid in a corn shock. He was not found and returned to his home.

Within a few days his wife died in childbirth. He was left with nine young children and an infant daughter.

Charles' sister took the newborn daughter into her home, and foster homes were found for the remaining children. Life went on.

My grandfather and his younger brother, boys in their early teens, were taken into a wealthy farmer's home. I have often wondered exactly how this came to happen.

My overactive imagination suggests that the farmer may have become acquainted with the barrel maker when he went to Bethel for his winter's supply of corn whiskey, for that was the custom of the time. Whiskey was purchased and supposedly used for medicinal purposes.

The farmer raised the two boys with his three daughters. Eventually there were 10 double cousins from the two families, including my mother. She well remembered her parents, grandparents and all of the good and bad times that came to pass.

Today members of these families are scattered from coast to coast. There are farmers and teachers, factory workers and preachers scattered far and wide. Family members served as soldiers in several wars supporting America.

Everyone in this family traces their roots to an 18-year-old immigrant who bravely set out in 1844 to search for a better way of life.

I think he found it.

Margaret Stout
Plevna, Missouri

A Stowaway's Fresh Start

Jacob Smith originally came from Prussian Germany, which is now Poland. The country was at war at about the time Jacob was 16. For fear of having to go to war, Jacob stowed away on a ship to America. Because he was a stowaway, no passenger list includes his name and no record of which ship he emigrated on exists. His parents did not come to America, and for fear of their safety, Jacob never revealed their names or where in Germany they lived. Jacob never told anyone when or where he changed his name after coming to America.

He settled in Pennsylvania, near Allentown, in an area known as Pennsylvania Dutch. He enlisted in the Union Army there when he was 17, serving one year before mustering out.

After his discharge from the army, he was united in marriage to Emmaline Glasser in Philadelphia, Pennsylvania. He moved to Verona, Missouri, living there for 10 years, in which time four children were born. Two died in infancy. Jacob later moved to Marinville, Missouri, where he took up the trade of shoe repair; he worked at it for the rest of his life. They lived in Marinville for several years, then moved to Aurora, Missouri, where they lived the rest of their lives. They are both buried in Maple Park Cemetery, Aurora, Missouri.

George Smith
Muskogee, Oklahoma

New Home Prone to Flooding

My folks came to the United States—my dad from Bavaria and my mom from Austria—to have a better life. My dad had to quit school after the fourth grade and study to become a tinner and roofer. They met here at a wedding. She was a bridesmaid and he played the accordion, which he had brought along with him to make a living, before he became a full-time tinner and roofer.

I remember my folks telling me why there were so many steps to climb at Ellis Island. They believed those who couldn't reach the top or were out of breath when they got there were sent back, as they probably had heart problems and couldn't work.

My hometown, Johnstown, named after a Mr. Johns, was a friendly place—no locked doors, etc. The various nationalities in Johnstown found work with the Bethlehem Steel and Ironworks and in the mines. My dad had to learn to communicate with his customers through his expressions, his hands, etc. They only spoke German with my two oldest sisters. When my sisters started speaking English in school, they decided they'd better learn English too. After that they only spoke German when they didn't want us to know what they were talking about!

I was baptized, and my first Holy Communion and confirmation took place at one of the oldest churches in the city. It had survived three floods and two devastating fires. I never questioned why we belonged to this church instead of one of the other two Catholic churches we passed on the way to ours; perhaps it was because ours was German.

Johnstown is in a valley, completely surrounded by mountains. My mom said that during the 1889 flood she was baking cakes in an outdoor stove. When the water began to rise, she grabbed the cakes and went up to the second floor, where she threw one over to the next house. She watched houses go by with people sitting on the roofs. At the end of the street was a big hole in which houses and people disappeared.

Our town flooded again in 1936. I was in the eighth grade, and the nun said, "Go home, as the water is already flooded under the bridge," so we climbed over the bridge and went home. That Sunday they set up a table in the upstairs hall, and before the priest said Mass there, he stood before his congregation and cried. I had never seen a man cry before and it touched me deeply.

My dad's business completely disappeared; the water came in the back door and went out the front, taking everything with it. We were thankful he had a truck, as the Red Cross gave work to men with trucks hauling all the goods, blankets, shoes, clothes, etc., which came in from all over the United States. We kids got our first pair of roller skates that some kind person sent along. We kids went up to the church and school every day, slapping jars of Vaseline on the grill work, trying to get the mud off. The next day it was back. At the school we sorted wet and muddy books, papers, etc., trying to save something. We worked every day so the school could open that September.

Margaret Esper
Romeo, Michigan

The Misplaced Money Belt

The year was 1881. My grandparents and their five children left Germany for America—Land of Opportunity—where their sons would not have to "goose step" in the Franco-Prussian War. They eventually landed in New York, then bought train passage to Dubuque, Iowa. The land office had given them maps of northwest Iowa, where homesteading land was available. Using some of the money from his money belt, Grandfather purchased a wagon, horses and supplies, then joined a wagon train crossing the Iowa prairie. It was in the midst of summer. One evening while camping by a cool, inviting stream, all enjoyed a refreshing swim. The next morning, nearly an hour after the wagon train had departed, my grandfather realized he no longer was wearing his money belt. He had taken it off by the stream the night before and forgotten to put it on again.

Taking one of his horses, he rode frantically back on the trail to the stream. There, hanging on a branch, swinging in the breeze, was the money belt—its contents so needed to buy supplies.

They bought homesteading rights in Clay County, Iowa. Three more children were born—including my mother. Some homesteaders lived in sod homes, but not my grandfather and his family. He and his sons built a log house. He insisted that his family learn English; no more German. They were thrifty, hard-working people. When Grandfather died in 1904 of typhoid fever he held considerable landownings and was a respected American citizen.

Joyce Fodness
Spirit Lake, Iowa

Descendants Spread Throughout the States

I am one of the many descendants of Conrad Lippard, a German farmer who immigrated to North America in 1738. His wife, Anna Martha, his son, Wilhelm, and his family came with him.

Disease, starvation, unsanitary conditions, accidents and storms at sea took a devastating toll on the ship's passengers, and more than half died before reaching their destination.

Conrad left Germany in the wake of French persecution to come to William Penn's New World colony. He settled near Philadelphia.

Conrad's son, Wilhelm, couldn't afford land in Pennsylvania, so he went to North Carolina in the 1750s in search of a better life. This was the beginning of the Conrad Lippard family scattering throughout the New World. My mother was a North Carolina Lippard.

Conrad's descendants are now scattered throughout the United States.

Jessie Kelly
Dalton City, Illinois

Newcomer Delighted by Fourth of July Celebration

My grandpa, William Schmidt, was born in Prussia. At the age of 8 he came with his family to America. They came on the sailing vessel *Charlotte*. After a voyage of nine weeks and three days, they landed in New York on July 3. The next day being the Fourth, Grandpa Schmidt was delighted by the celebrations and activities.

When Grandpa Schmidt was 13 years old, both of his parents had died. He had to take his place as a wage earner and do a man's work from then on. He worked for farmers in Lyon County, Iowa, and later bought a farm in Wheeler Township. The farm was purchased in 1881 for $1,000: $6.25 per acre for the entire 160-acre farm.

Myrtle May Duin
George, Iowa

Not So Rich After All

My grandmother, Elizabeth Gammeringer, came from Messtettin, Germany, alone when she was 18. Her relatives got the $80 together for her passage over. She arrived by way of Ellis Island with "over $7, but less than $8." She knew only two English words. I often heard her say, "All I knew in English was 'yes' and 'no,' and I kept getting those mixed up."

The man who processed her papers felt sorry for Grandmother and offered her a home with his family. He paid her $2 a week to help his wife with the housework and children. She stayed with this family for about two years and learned the language. My German grandfather had lost his wife and was left with four small children. He put an ad in the paper for a German housekeeper. My grandmother, then 20 years old, answered the ad; they were married in 1902. He was Nicholas Meyer, son of Christoff and Helena Meyer, from Trier, Germany.

My grandmother said that her relatives thought that everyone in America was rich. They planned for her to send money for all of them to come over when she got to America. She did have a sister that came over later.

I visited some relatives in Germany a couple of years ago, one of whom had a letter from my grandmother, written after she had been over here awhile. She told how disappointed she was to find everyone in America was not rich and ended by saying, "I even have to wash my husband's overalls."

She came here at 18 and died at 83. All her life she pronounced her "th's" as though they were "d's": dis, dat, dem, dose, etc.

Melba Meyer Wiggins
Paden, Oklahoma

Not Everyone Adjusted to America

My husband's family came to the United States from Germany in 1912, which was during Ellis Island's peak years. The Dingler family consisted of father; mother; two daughters, ages 12 and 6; and twin sons, 9 years old. The father had learned the locksmith and machinist trades and was employed in a shop in Durlach, Baden.

Descendants of the family do not know whether the parents were contemplating and intending to emigrate from Germany to far-off America. However, an acquaintance of the family entertained a guest from Abilene, Kansas, who portrayed to her host family and the Dinglers a picture of opportunity and potential in the United States. Perhaps she described to these families the Swiss-German town of Enterprise, southeast of Abilene, with a flourishing flour mill and a large, progressive machine shop. Both industries were owned and managed by German-speaking Swiss immigrants.

It is believed the visitor encouraged both families to accompany her to America, which they did. She served as their escort and guide, since she could speak and understand both German and English.

In all probability there were mixed emotions as the two families prepared to leave kinfolk and friends, as well as familiar surroundings—likely never to return—to make a new life in a strange and unknown world. Good-byes were painful and difficult. Clothing, a few dishes, some personal items, and the family Bible were all the belongings they could carry with them. They traveled by train from Durlach to the departure port, Hamburg, where they boarded the ocean liner, *President Grant*.

One of the 9-year-old twins had a vivid memory of delicious fresh-baked bread rolls coming out of the oven and cooling near the deck. He and other children aboard helped themselves but were reprimanded by the ship's baker. After 11 days of viewing only sky and water, the sight of the Statute of Liberty and New York Harbor left an everlasting impression on these travelers. The ship docked the evening they arrived, but not until the following morning were the passengers permitted to disembark.

Ellis Island's huge Registry Room was the nation's primary reception depot for immigrants awaiting questioning by inspectors. These families were among the great majority of steerage passengers, and the New World was uncertain and unpredictable to them. After the group passed the Ellis Island scrutiny, they found their way to another room of the Registry Building, where they purchased railroad tickets for the long overland train ride to Abilene. The 6-year-old daughter recalled arriving in Abilene during the night. They stayed a week or so. The father got a job at the shops, and the family moved to the village of Enterprise.

About six months later the parents separated. The father and one twin returned to Germany. The mother, with full responsibility for providing for herself and the three children, remained in Enterprise. Money was a scarce commodity, and life was a lot of hard work, but as time passed the children assumed responsibilities.

The children attended school in Enterprise. Nine-year-old Herman recalled repeating the first grade because he couldn't speak English, but these children eventually did learn the language. The principal of the school was sympathetic toward the family and helped bridge their language barriers; he too could speak German. The children taught their mother the new words they learned at school. She too mastered the language by learning to read, write and speak it.

The young boy's first paying job was running errands and watering a local widow's horse for the tidy sum of 25 cents per week. This lad worked as a day laborer on a nearby farm for a few years, and as soon as his age allowed he began working as an apprentice at the shop that had hired his father for several months. Enterprise was this man's home for the remainder of his life, and he was an employee of the local "shops" for 50 years.

Helen C. Dingler
Enterprise, Kansas

Grandmother's Strength Remembered

Elizabeth Shearer Hartzel, my great-grandmother on my father's side, was born March 27, 1836, in Hesser, Germany. She had to be a strong person.

Great-Grandma Hartzel came to the United States alone, because she was to be indentured to a couple who wanted a maid.

While she was on the boat to the United States, the husband of the couple who had sponsored her died. When she arrived, the deceased man's widow could not keep her.

She somehow got to Erie, Pennsylvania, where she married and lived.

I was about 2 when she died. I'm not sure whether I actually remember her or whether I just remember pictures of her and what members of our family have told me. She died September 4, 1926.

Arlene Futrell
Stokes, North Carolina

Heritage Came in Handy

When my ancestors came to America, Grandpa Finkenbinder said to his children, "We are in America now—we shall speak English!" However, they must have spoken some German; a few of the words were passed on to me by my father. As I grew up, my father told me that I was speaking Dutch. When I became an adult we had a lesson in Home Demonstration Club—now known as FCE (Family, Community Education Club)—about the Pennsylvania Dutch ancestry. I learned there were many Pennsylvania Dutch who had German ancestry. My German was called the low German; my husband spoke high German.

My grandfather and great-uncle ran a store in Friend, Kansas, in the early 1900s. A group of immigrants settled north of Scott City, Kansas. They could speak very little English.

There were two grocery stores in Friend. The mother and daughter of one of the immigrant families came to my grand-father's store and wanted to purchase a *thinnerhoop*. Grandpa went and got them a thimble. The woman jumped with glee! She had found a merchant who could speak and understand her language. It seems she was able to purchase items at the other store and she was going to take them back. Grandpa convinced her to keep the items, but she could come to his store from now on. This proved America was the Land of Opportunity for this immigrant family.

I am proud I was able to glean a small part of my ancestry from my forefathers who came to the Land of Opportunity. Because of what I learned, I was able to help in a church contest. A Sunday School teacher had a scavenger hunt for her class. One of the items to find was someone who could sing a German song. One of the students came to the class I was attending and asked if anyone could sing a German song. I said I could. Everyone was so surprised, as no one in the church realized I was of German descent. I had to sing the song for them. Later, the minister had me sing it for him.

Yes, my folks found opportunity in America when Pennsylvania was being settled.

Pauline Fecht
Syracuse, Kansas

A Visit to the Homestead

My father came to America when he was 11 years old. He never said too much about how he came or anything about the trip, but we were told stories when we visited my father's birthplace in Germany in 1972. We were able to locate an elderly couple, Johann and Hermina Gelder, both in their 80s. After the shock of someone coming from America to see them was over, they told us the following story. They remembered well my grandmother leaving with her children to go to America. Her husband had died, leaving my grandmother to raise five children alone. Two older children had already left Germany for America, and they told her she should come, too, as things were so much better. Johann and Hermina remembered that Grandma sold everything she had, including her food, by going up and down the streets of Lucthenburg, Ostfriesland, Germany, to gather money to leave her homeland with her five children. In 1905, six years after my grandfather died, she left Germany with my father and his four sisters. We remember the German relatives saying that they never heard from them again; it was as though Grandmother Gelder and her children had disappeared from the face of the earth. To say Mr. and Mrs. Gelder were happy to see us and learn about my family is an understatement. Johann told us that he and my father, Dirk, went to school together. I will always cherish the memories of this trip when my wife and I were able to walk the village streets where my father was born, lived and played.

Leonard Gelder
Wellsburg, Iowa

Artisan from the Old World

The immigration story of my father's family is lost in the mists of time. My dad was of Welsh descent, born in 1873 on a farm in Owen County, Kentucky. His name was Lewis Marion Jones. Never was there a more Welsh name, or one more difficult to trace. One can only guess at how many Welsh families were named Jones.

Dad's mother, whose maiden name was Schooler, died when he was an infant. He was raised in Indiana by his mother's brother, John Henry Schooler, and his wife, Rebecca. How I wish I had asked for more information about that family when I had the opportunity!

My maternal grandparents emigrated from Germany in the 1860s. My mother, born in 1889, was their youngest. She and her siblings were first-generation United States citizens. One of her brothers, John M. Schmid, became circulation director of all the Hearst newspapers and a president of the International Circulation Managers Association.

My dear Aunt Rose lived in our home for 20 years. She wrote, in her beautiful penmanship, an interesting account of our ancestral background; the following information is from her record.

My great-great-grandfather was a Royal District Forester in Bavaria. His daughter, of German and French descent, married a horticulturist and copper engraver who owned a large estate and a hotel named *Zum Hirsch*, "The Stag." They had 14 children, including two sets of twins. Ten lived to adulthood, and several of the sons were skilled artisans, working in gold, ivory, ebony, tortoise-shell and mother-of-pearl jewelry.

My grandfather learned his trade as a journeyman tinner, and was probably the only family member to come to the United States. He and my grandmother-to-be were schoolchildren together. They were taught French in school, but spoke German. He came to the United States first, then sent for his fiancée. They were married in

Cincinnati in 1869. My grandmother was of German and Hungarian descent. Her father was a craftsman of musical instruments.

Our family heirlooms include a tortoise-shell pin with an intricate mother-of-pearl design, and an ivory pin of carved angels. There is also a delicate silver filigree box about the size of a quarter, which once contained a ducat, a European gold coin, given to my grandmother on a special occasion.

Those early immigrants, forebears of us all, were adventuresome, courageous, energetic and willing to win. Today we need the same qualities to face the new wave of immigrants storming for admittance to the good old USA!

Marcia Baker Pogue
Cincinnati, Ohio

Hilly Land Preferred to Flat

Timon Young, my great-great-grandfather, who was said to have been a driver for the kaiser of Germany, immigrated to America from Germany in 1851 at the age of 27. He lived in New York until 1855, when he married Eva Kolb, a native Bavarian. After they were married they traveled by train to Chariton, Iowa. The hack driver wanted $8 to take them to Garden Grove, Iowa, a distance of about 20 miles. They had only $5, so they decided to save their money and walk the distance in one day, carrying their few possessions over their shoulders in a red pocket handkerchief. After arriving in Garden Grove, Timon was able to borrow enough money to purchase a small home; with subsequent purchases he kept adding land until he owned a fine farm. It is said by family that the original homestead was good flat Iowa farmland near Garden Grove, but Timon, wanting more water, traded it for a hill farm with a spring.

Ann Wyer
Corydon, Iowa

"I Hope We Will Land in Good Shape"

Norddeutscher Lloyd Bremen
An Bord des D., Dresden
Febr. 28, Mar. 1

Dear Sophie,

Your nice letter I received and it was good. It was a pleasure on the first day on board of ship to hear from you. I didn't expect that.

Now I am going to fulfill your wish and write you a few words. I hope you are okay. We experienced a lot here already.

The twentieth of Febr. the ship went to sea at Twelve o'clock noon.

I found company with some young girls and a married couple.

The first night I slept good until Sunday morning I couldn't even stand up anymore. I was so seasick. I had to stay in bed on Sunday and below they were dancing. The next morning it was better. We landed twice, Febr. 21, at 6 o'clock in Scherbourg, France and on Febr. 22 at 4:00 P.M. in Ireland. There we saw land and that was great.

Monday we had a storm and at times very windy. We could not be on deck very much.

Last night we had a costume festival. Then we danced.

Today I'll finish the letter. I think we will be in Halifax. We will let those on board who are going to Canada. Tomorrow evening we will be in New York. Monday early we'll go on land. Then will be the train ride.

Now I'll write your parents and my family. Now I hope we will land in good shape.

Greetings
from Elisabeth Holscher
Submitted by Olga Feyerherm
West Point, Nebraska

Great-Grandparents Survived Train Disaster

My great-grandparents on my grandmother's side came from Germany. Asmus Stoltenberg was born September 29, 1842, at

Stackendorf, Schleswig-Holstein, Germany. Dorothea Weise was born October 18, 1837. Asmus became a naturalized citizen in Scott County, Iowa, on February 16, 1870.

Asmus and Dorothea worked as servants or laborers in the same home. As I understand, he came to America to avoid forceful conscription in the German Army.

Unmarried, they arrived in New York aboard the ship *Neckar*, then boarded a train of the Grand Trunk Railroad line. This train, which was scheduled to go through Canada and the western United States, carried 475 immigrants from different European countries.

On June 29, 1864, this train fell through the open Richlieu Drawbridge at St. Hillaire, near Montreal, Canada. Eighty-seven bodies were recovered from the ruins; an additional 80 were wounded. Some of the train cars had landed on a barge below the bridge. Without the barge to prevent the cars from plunging into the river, more persons would have drowned. The immigrants' various origins and virtual anonymity made it impossible to correctly identify the dead. Fortunately, Asmus and Dorothea were not injured. They continued on to Iowa and were married at Davenport on August 2, 1864.

In 1876, a group of men bought 11,647 acres of land in Ida County, Iowa, from the Northwestern Railroad at $5.75 an acre. Asmus settled there and is referred to as the first settler in Ida County, Iowa—the German settlement at Holstein, Iowa. His wife and family arrived later. He eventually bought five more farms for his six living children.

I am proud of what is behind me, and I hope to learn more about my heritage. I know my ancestors would be proud of my family—four very well-educated daughters, and a son who retired after years in the army.

Marian B. Williams
Fair Oaks, Indiana

Immigrants Sought Life Free of Famine and War

The middle of the 19th century was a time of political unrest in Europe, and many thousands of young people and entire families left to seek better futures in the United States. A flood of immigrants, especially Germans and Irish, settled in the greater Cincinnati area during this time.

The Prussians overran Germany and forced every unmarried young man between the ages of 21-25 to serve in the Prussian army as it swept into France and continued its goal of conquering all of Europe.

When Josef Vater turned 21, he had just dislocated his shoulder and been given a three-month deferment. He took advantage of this postponement to book passage on the freighter *Wieland* from the port of Bremen, Germany. The ship's register listed him as 26 instead of 21; we can only surmise he lied about his age to avoid being questioned about leaving the country while of draft age. His profession was listed as wagon maker and his destination was Ohio.

He traveled by train from New York Harbor to Cincinnati and arrived with just $5 in his pocket. As was the custom at that time, large landowners met the trains and offered jobs to the immigrants. Josef went home with one and worked for him for several years as he saved money and learned to speak English.

Four years after arriving, he sent word back to his family in Berlin that he would pay for the transportation of any brother or sister who wanted to join him in America. His sister Margaret, who was only 17, accepted the offer and came here to live.

During the Prussian oppression of Germany, Ireland was in the depths of its deepest famine and depression. The history books refer to it as "the potato famine of the 1840s and '50s." There had been severe drought for many years and crops, especially potatoes—their main food and export crop—had failed. Thousands of young people left the country in search of a better life in America:

Julia Corbett was one of them. She and her three sisters, all in their late teens and early 20s, came to the States together. They, too, lived with and worked for people here while saving their money and learning the ways of their new homeland. Language was not a problem, since they already spoke English.

Julia and Josef worked for the same family. They eventually married and bought a farm of their own in northern Kentucky, across the river from Cincinnati. They had 10 children and celebrated their 50th wedding anniversary three years before Julia died in 1917. The road running past their farm is still known as Vater Road.

In this mechanized world, where remote controls simplify life, we often lose sight of the struggles and hardships our ancestors endured to settle in this land of promise.

Elizabeth Vater Florence
Butler, Kentucky

American Roots Ran Deep

Great-grandmother was born in Hanover, Germany. Her parents were very poor people who had a hard time caring for their children.

When she was very young, Grandmother's parents hired her out to a well-to-do family. There she had the status of a lowly servant girl, doing all the household's menial tasks for her keep. Her bed was in a cold corner of the dark attic, and board consisted of leftovers uneaten by the family. She got a few hand-me-downs for clothing. After working for several years she was paid wages— a few cents per week. Once a month she could visit her family. The walk home was long, but along the way she gathered edible greens to contribute to the home folks' meal.

She met and fell in love with John, an ambitious young man whose dream was to someday go to America. They had been married only a short time when John announced he had saved enough to buy passage to the United States. Grandmother would continue to work until he sent for her. After many long months, a letter came with a ticket for her ocean voyage.

Grandmother made a last visit to bid her parents good-bye. It was sad to realize she would probably never see them again.

Grandmother decided she would greet John in style. She sacrificed a few hard-earned pennies and bought a new hat. It was a beautiful creation of velvet, ribbon and plumes. She was so proud of it, and she hoped John would be proud of her.

The hat was the first thing John noticed. "Come, we will buy you a beautiful new hat—that one looks like the old country." With that, he pulled out her hatpins and tossed her cherished bonnet into the harbor.

The next shock came when John said, "Now we will go and be married." Grandmother protested, saying surely they were legally married in Germany.

"Oh, yes," he said. "But now we are in this new country, and we will be married the American way."

Years later, Grandmother's marriage ended sadly when John abandoned her and the children and returned to the old country. Grandmother's American roots were deep by then, and she stayed to raise her children and become a successful businesswoman.

A story came back from Germany after World War I that caused Grandmother much unhappiness. She learned that her own mother had died of starvation during the desperate times the German people endured. That was so hard for Grandmother to bear. She was one who always took delight in cooking good food for those she loved.

She was a loyal, hard-working woman. I will always be proud to claim her as my own great-grandmother.

Jean Kristiansen
Nashua, Iowa

The Magic Pullet Eggs

When pullets are 5 months old they begin to lay—first small eggs, then, for the rest of their lives, they lay regular-sized eggs. It was these first small eggs that my great-grandmother called the *magic eien*—magic eggs. She believed that when pullets first began to lay, there was a special quality about their eggs—a life ingredient.

Great-Grandmother was born long ago on a large duchy in Germany. When she was very young she was assigned to be a goose girl, and every day she watched and guarded the geese. It was a very pleasant way of living. At Christmas the duke and duchess held an open house for their peasantry, and all went to the castle for the big holiday party. Great-Grandmother must have been a very pretty little girl because the duchess singled her out to dance for the people. The fiddlers tuned up and Great-Grandmother did her little dance, but ran and hid behind her mother's skirts during the resultant applause.

When Great-Grandmother was about 16 she fell in love with one of the duke's stableboys. His name was Johan Guhse, and he was a favorite of the duke because he had a good touch with the fine horses in the stables. The young couple married and were happy except for one thing—they couldn't seem to have any babies.

The great wars came, and the duke was killed in battle. The duchy fell on hard times and the peasants often went hungry. Johan and Gussie could see no future for themselves, so one day Gussie dressed in her best and went to see the duchess. The duchess had become very old and sad, but she remembered Gussie. Gussie still worked with the geese, but Johan was worried because there were no fine horses left in the castle barns. The old duchess questioned Gussie about what they wanted to do, and Gussie told her they wanted to go to the new land, America, and raise geese. The old duchess shook her head. She motioned Gussie closer and whispered in her ear. Then she dug down into the old bag that hung at her waist—very thin now and almost empty—giving Gussie enough money to buy the young couple's passage to America.

It was a long, hard sea journey in steerage, but they finally came to the new land, following others to the state of Wisconsin where they settled. The young couple worked for others until they had saved enough money to buy a small acreage. Did Gussie raise geese? No, she followed the duchess's advice and bought chickens. When the young pullets started laying, Gussie was so busy with her chickens and the gardening that she was almost four months pregnant before she realized the old duchess' secret had worked. They had four children before Great-Grandfather Guhse became blind. People said he had worked too long in the duke's stables, where the miasma of horse manure and urine had caused his eyes to fail, but today we realize that he probably had cataracts. He died in his 50s, but Great-Grandmother Guhse lived on until she was nearly 100. She always kept a few chickens, and she treasured the young pullet's first eggs—the *magic eien*—and gave them away to young women whenever she could. She always told them that there was life in the new pullet eggs. "*Sehr gut!* Very good," she said.

Do you suppose Great-Grandmother Guhse was right?

Evelyn Holden
Lebanon, Oregon

Family Lost Dream but Held Together

The century was new as 15-year-old Martha and 16-year-old Minnie Claussen set sail across the ocean to the Land of Opportunity. They arrived in New York with the grand sum of 15 cents between them and train tickets to Davenport, Iowa. Thanks to the other travelers, they didn't go hungry.

A cousin met their train and provided them with employment on his farm. The Claussen girls went to work to earn money to send back to their parents in Schleswig-Holstein, Germany. There was no longer any farmland available in that area; so Father Ludwig, Mother Christina, and their eight children dreamed of the opportunities the New World would provide.

They finally raised enough money for their passage. Johann "John," the oldest son, stayed behind in Germany to fulfill his military obligation. Grandma and Grandpa Claussen, along with Detlaf "Dave," Gustaf "Gus," Ludwig Daniel "Louie" (my father), Emil, Bertha and my Great-Grandmother Lorenz arrived at Ellis Island on March 1, 1903. The problems that arose during their processing were terrifying. The fear of having to get back on the ship and return to Germany was very real. Older people were not being admitted into this country. Somehow they convinced the immigration official that my Great-Grandmother Lorenz would not become a financial burden to this new land. Her family assured them that they would provide for her.

Joyfully the family headed for Davenport, Iowa, where Martha and Minnie waited for them. Grandpa Claussen died within the year. The family's dream of owning its own dairy farm was shattered.

Grandma, being of sturdy German stock, held the family together. They grew a garden, and with the aid of a hand cart, she and the boys peddled fresh vegetables door to door, up and down the streets of Davenport. Grandma hired the boys out to milk cows for other farmers. The money the boys earned they gave to Grandma to provide for the family.

The Claussen children grew up to become good United States citizens. Dave, Gus and Louie worked for the Red Jacket Manufacturing Company. Emil became a commercial artist. Only John became a farmer. He worked on farms in the Davenport area but decided he wanted a farm of his own. The farms in Iowa were all too expensive, so he headed for South Dakota, where he homesteaded near Hayes.

Beverly Claussen Caviness
Greenfield, Iowa

Family Immigrated Twice

Between the years 1763-1862, hundreds of Germans migrated from Germany to German settlements in Russia.

Catherine the Great of Russia was German. She knew what excellent farmers the German people were and that Russia needed to populate the southern areas of her country.

She offered the Germans tax-free land and promised that their young men would not have to serve in the Russian Army. She even guaranteed that they would be able to practice their religion.

This manifesto came at a critical time for the Germans. Napoleon's Army had recently swept through, taking many men and boys with them. There had been severe crop failures for several years. Like America's early pioneers, men were looking for a better life for their families, even though it meant saying good-bye to all that was familiar and taking a long, difficult trip into the unknown.

In spite of all the promises of aid on the part of the Russian government, the initial years were fraught with great difficulties. The long trek itself, under the prevailing conditions, made in-human demands upon the first immigrants. Some of them had to travel more than 2,000 miles. At the time of settlement there was a woeful lack of dwellings, farming equipment and draught animals. It took time to get used to the climate and to the new, totally different farming methods in the vast, treeless Steppes.

Joining these brave pilgrims at this dramatic time in history were some of my early ancestors. They settled in the Black Sea area near Odessa, Russia.

Before Grandma, Eva Marguerite Hirning, and Grandpa, Adam Grenz, married, each had lost their mates through death. Grand-ma's first husband died when their third baby was 3 months old.

By the time they made their decision to come to "the Land of Opportunity," they had her three children, his two children, and their first little girl, 2-year-old Elizabeth.

It is difficult to imagine the scene before they left Russia. Grandma's relatives held a funeral for her because they knew they would never see her alive again! How hard it must have been to leave their loved relatives and friends.

Grandma and Grandpa landed in Baltimore, Maryland, on May 15, 1887. Seven days later, Grandmother gave birth to their son, John, in Palmer, Iowa. What must it have been like to have a baby only one week after arriving in a strange land? They probably spoke no English. Did Grandma have the baby alone? Did kindly women of the town help? There were six other children with them to be washed, fed and looked after.

They stayed in Palmer for eight days and then moved on to South Dakota, where Grandfather's brother lived. Perhaps they heard of greater opportunities, because they went west to Oregon after 11 months.

Grandpa was a brick mason by trade, and his work can still be seen in buildings in Salem, Oregon.

Eventually they moved to a farm.

They had seven children, including my handsome dad, Lee Andrew Grenz.

Grandpa died in 1900, a few months before their seventh child was born.

In my memory, I see Grandmother, a tiny, slender woman, about 5 feet 1 inch tall, with white hair and blue eyes. She usually wore an apron with white peppermints in the pocket. I remember her rolling out noodle dough and cutting it very fast into slender strands.

Grandma died in 1943 when she was 87.

I shall always be grateful that my ancestors had the courage to come to America. I am proud of them.

Nyla Booth
Beaverton, Oregon

Man Traveled to America in a Barrel

When I was a child in the '30s, many of the older men who attended our Lutheran Church in the country had emigrated from Europe. This was back when men and women entered by separate doors and sat on separate sides of the church!

One little old man with a long, white beard and heavy German accent always fascinated me. I was told that when he came here from Germany, he floated over in a barrel! I now realize this was probably a joke. Maybe he floated from the boat to shore, but there's no way he floated across the ocean in a barrel!

During all my growing-up years, whenever I saw this man, I immediately pictured him standing upright in a wooden barrel, holding on with both hands, his long beard whipping in the wind while the barrel floated gently up and down with the waves.

Elaine Derendinger
Franklin, Missouri

Mixed Reactions to America

My grandfather, August Maiwald, was born in a tiny hamlet in Silesia, then part of Germany. His parents each had children by previous marriages; the high mortality rate of the times led to many marriages of convenience. There were no jobs for women, and men were unsuited for caring for children. As the youngest of the lot, Grandfather was the target of abuse. He often said, "When my mother's kids weren't beating on me, my father's were."

Apprenticed to a miller at 13, August had to carry heavy sacks of grain up the narrow stairs to the mill tower hoppers, where it would feed down to the grindstones that reduced it to flour. He could take only short naps on a pile of grain sacks, because the hopper emptied every half hour. He finished his training in 1867, only to find that city mills, with their steam-powered steel rollers, were replacing the water-powered gristmills.

Fortunately—or perhaps unfortunately—August was drafted into the Prussian cavalry as a *hussar*, a light horseman. He got three years of harsh training, then was sent to fight against the French in the Franco-Prussian War of 1870-71. While scouting ahead of a supply train, he ran into an ambush, where it was kill or be killed. The iron ring in his cap kept the enemy's saber cut from splitting his skull, but he carried the scar to his grave. He was given a lead bullet to bite when his scalp was sewn up without anesthetic. While nearly biting the bullet in two, he made a pact with God, vowing that if he survived the war unharmed, no son of his would ever fight or die for the glory of the fatherland.

After the war, August was stung by the wanderlust bug. He hiked through the lovely Bavarian countryside, working sporadically, drifting ever onward, sleeping in haystacks and seeing new sights. It was then that he met a beautiful woman who regarded him as her knight in shining armor.

That was my grandmother, Rosina Bartnig. Her mother, widowed at 30 with three children, married an old skinflint who kept even raw potatoes and carrots locked up so his wife's brats could have only the miserable few he doled out. He often told his drinking buddies, "I'd buy the old woman some liverwurst, but she would only give it to her brats!" Rosina and August met while picking up potatoes in her stepfather's potato field. Realizing that the old curmudgeon would never let her go because she was such a good worker, the young lovers eloped that very night. Rosina kissed her sleeping mother and brothers good-bye, wrapped a few things in her Sunday dress, then the barefoot couple ran away in the night.

They were married by an Evangelical minister in 1878. August got a small hardscrabble farm in Silesia, but then the government helped him get a larger farm in Posen, now Posnan, Poland.

Their first child, Alma, was born in 1878, and Carl was born in 1879. My father, Frederick "Fritz," was born in 1884 and his sister

Anna in 1892. Their home, like all the others, was a house-barn, where the cattle lived in one end and folks in the other. All the milk from their three cows was made into butter to be sold, leaving them only the sour buttermilk. No chickens or eggs could be eaten; like the fat hogs and geese they raised, all had to go to market to pay the taxes and mortgage, plus a few luxuries such as salt, pepper and sugar, things we take for granted.

When my Uncle Carl was 16, Grandpa sent him to the States to avoid the draft. Five years later, at great sacrifice, he sent my dad. Unable to run his farm without the boys' help, he sold his land and moved to Berlin, where he found work as a carpenter's helper.

The rattletrap train that took young Fritz to Berlin seemed a mechanical marvel to him. He stayed there with an uncle for a week, over-awed by the city's beautiful museums and gardens. He was put on the train to Hamburg, where he took a ship across the English Channel to Grimsby. Then the youngster took a train to the mighty port of Liverpool. There he was herded from the train depot, along with the other emigrants, to the blowsy old *Pretoria* of the Hamburg-American Line. After two weeks afloat in steerage, where the seasick moaned all night, unable to eat the pig slop food and pounded by heavy seas, young Fritz was thrilled to see the Statue of Liberty. He was shoved through Ellis Island, had his eyelids pulled up with a buttonhook to check for trachoma and was fed with hundreds of others at a long table. His brother Carl met him to take him to Providence, Rhode Island. Then they boarded a trolley to Carl's home in Darlington, a suburb of Pawtucket.

There, Fritz met Carl's wife Clara and daughter Edith. He was astonished at the nutritious food and lack of formality. White bread, two eggs and coffee cake, all at the same meal? Astounding! He fell in love with America on the spot. He boarded with his brother and got a job next day in the monstrous Royal Weaving Factory, the largest silk mill in the world. Fritz wandered about the city, astonished at such things as ice cream, amusement parks and the swarms of folks in the stores, as well as the zoo, the theaters and the baseball games, where the players got only free beer as their pay.

Young Fritz joined the church, opened a savings account and went to night school to learn proper English. Five years later, when he became a citizen, he went back to Germany to persuade his parents to come to America. His mother finally agreed, providing Fritz waited until his kid sister Anna was confirmed in the Evangelical church. He went back to his old village for a visit before bringing his folks to the promised land.

My other grandfather, Franz Bauer, was born in 1847 in Bavaria, Germany. He was the oldest of 11 children and was put to weaving silk at age 9. We know nothing more of his early life or when he and his first wife came to America. She disliked America so much she leaped to her death from their apartment window, leaving Franz with Otto, their 8-year-old son. Otto never got over her death and could not get along with his stepmother. He ran away when he was 14 and 15, leaving for good at 16.

Grandma Bauer, Mary Siegle, was born in Bavaria in 1865. Her father died when she was 3, and her mother remarried three weeks later. Her stepfather was a winemaker. He drank too much of his own stuff and became violent when he was soused, which was about once a week. At 15, Mary took a position as a maid/companion to a wealthy German woman who brought Mary to New York's society scene. Mary absorbed quite a bit of culture from this fine lady, but quit when the husband became too demanding. She met and married the widowed Franz Bauer in January of 1892 and bore him a daughter, Annie, on November 24th of that year. She was my mother. Her brother Frank was born May 16, 1902.

When Frank was born, Grandma took my mom out of school and turned Frank over to her to raise. At 11, my mother had sole responsibility for her brother and all the housework while her mother cooked and made their clothes on her old shuttle Singer sewing machine. When Frank started school, Annie pestered her father to get her a job, so he took her to the Royal Weaving Factory with him and taught her the weaving trade.

She became friendly with young Anna Maiwald who got her a date with her brother, Fred. That's how my parents met. They had a chaste three-year engagement, then married on January 24, 1912.

I was born August 31, 1913, during a violent thunderstorm. It was a Sunday, so Pop was there to assist the doctor. They laid Mom on the kitchen table, so Doc Lelond could use his forceps—I still have the scars. Doc gave Pop the nod to give Mom a whiff of chloroform. Lightning hit the old oxheart cherry tree in the backyard and there I was, all 10 and one-half pounds of me. Ta-dah! The total cost of my entry into the world was $8.

Carl W. Maiwald
Pine Bush, New York

A Memorable First Sentence in English

My grandfather, George Ubbinga, was born in Germany and came to America with his parents in 1884. They first lived in McComb, Illinois. As soon as they arrived, 17-year-old George secured work in a brick factory in a small town near McComb. This was a Yankee settlement, and no one spoke or understood German. Grandpa felt insecure and spoke nothing more than an occasional word while he was at work, but he picked up words and phrases here and there. One night he left his jacket at work, and when he went to pick it up the next morning, rats had gotten into it and ruined it. Very angry, he exploded, "Damn the American rats!" The sudden outburst from this quiet boy so surprised and amused his fellow workers that it was never forgotten. His first sentence in English became a much quoted, good-humored byword among those he worked with as long as he was there.

Myrtle May Duin
George, Iowa

Brothers Spent 61 Years in America

Rolf Jacob Fecht of Wiessens, Germany, and Fentke Maria Jansses of Holtrop, Germany, were married April 16, 1893, in the German Lutheran Church in Bremenhol, Germany.

On August 21, 1890, Rolf Jacob Fecht received a citation from the German Army for his excellent marksmanship. After his service in the army, he wanted to go to America, where some of his relatives had gone. Rolf was afraid he would have to go back in the army again, and he didn't want any part of it.

On April 28, 1893, Rolf, his bride, Fentke, and younger brother, Albert, 16, set sail for America, arriving at the Port of Baltimore on the steamship *Dresden.*

The family went to Carthage, Illinois. Their entire family was born in the United States. The first seven children were born in or around Carthage, Hancock County, Illinois. The family moved from Illinois in 1907, relocating around Wilcox, Nebraska. Later they moved to the Huntley, Nebraska, area. The last four children were born in Nebraska.

Albert Jacob Fecht, the 16-year-old immigrant, married Anna Katherine Helmrich on February 12, 1902, at Camp Point, Illinois. In 1907, Albert and Anna moved with Rolf's family to Wilcox, Nebraska, and later moved to Caney, Kansas.

The two brothers, Rolf Jacob and Albert Jacob Fecht, who came to the United States together, were again united in death. Rolf and Albert passed away at the same hour, day and year: Tuesday, July 13, 1954, at 9:30 a.m. Services were conducted on the following Friday, one in Nebraska and the other in Kansas.

These two brothers spent 61 years in America and never returned to their homeland, Germany, for even a visit.

Pauline Fecht
Syracuse, Kansas

Crossed the Atlantic on a Cattle Boat

My Great-Grandfather John left the state of Prussia in northern Germany at 14 to begin a new life where, "You can get good job and make a lot of money."

Obtaining a job on a cattle boat, his journey to the Land of Opportunity began in 1864. There were also human passengers on board the large sailing ship.

Sailing speed depended entirely on wind force. During the voyage, winds were less than expected, lengthening the trip.

Food supplies were running low. Grain and hay for the cattle ran out. Consequently some of the livestock died. People became ill. The cattle carcasses were skinned and butchered, giving the crew and passengers fresh meat, which sustained them the rest of the way.

Although my great-grandfather knew no one in the United States and spoke no English, he found a job soon after reaching his new homeland. "I was so happy to be in this country, I would do anything."

Later, he met Sophia, also an immigrant from Germany. They married and raised a family: two boys and four girls.

Enjoying a long, successful life, he died at 92 in Oklahoma.

Janice I. Kinman
Carthage, Missouri

Keeping Tradition Alive

America! Were the stories really true? A person could work at the profession of his choosing and could worship God—in freedom.

I had learned from childhood that our ancestor Abraham had been promised by God that he would be the father of a great nation. Maybe that was to be America! Political unrest was great in Prussia following the Napoleonic Wars. The grand alliance of Prussia, Austria and Russia fought amongst itself. Prussia did not receive the constitution that its citizens desired. Even though

Jews were given equal status in politics and business I did not trust men with political power. In May 1848, the National Assembly met in Frankfurt. It adopted a Bill of Rights and wrestled earnestly with the problem of German unity, even as uprisings in various parts of the country were put down by troops. Knowing some of the participants, fearing knowledge of some of my past activities and being of Jewish background, I feared for my life. I did not believe in expandist wars—taking human life to expand one's borders—I believed in the sanctity of life. After all, I was studying medicine to practice the profession of my fathers before me: It was tradition!

Although I knew the heartache of breaking family ties, I still made plans to take refuge in America. In 1862 Prince Otto von Bismarck was appointed President of the Council of Ministers by the Prussian king. This unscrupulous man would serve the cause of a united Germany, a very powerful state. So why stay in Prussia? Tradition? I would continue my family's tradition in America! My mother was a nurse, as was one of her sisters. My family had always been involved with medicine. I would go where there was freedom to voice dissent, and freedom to worship as Father Abraham did.

Landing in New York during 1869, I traveled to Omaha, Nebraska, with a family I had met on the ship. They were meeting some cousins who had homesteaded farms in Nebraska. Being farmers, they wanted their fair share of some of that rich soil. That part of the country had not been involved in the great Civil War. War again! Here it was brother against brother.

Needing money to finance my medical schooling, I found work in a tobacco store owned by a man named Herman Meyer. He was married, and he and his wife Cecelia had two boys, Adolph and Joseph. A third son, Henry, was born the same year Herman was killed in a tragic accident. I had resumed my medical studies that year, but I felt so sorry for Cecelia that I returned and managed the business for her until she could handle it. She was not business minded, and this was her only source of income. After a period of mourning, I asked her if she would consider marriage and letting me help her raise the boys. It wasn't a hard decision, as we were fond of each other, so we were married March 15, 1870. Now that I was settled, the difficult part was not being able to complete medical school. But I would have a son and send him to keep tradition alive in the Rich family.

Omaha was a thriving new community, bustling with commerce and trade from new settlers on the prairies. There was freight from the riverboats, and the Union Pacific Railroad that spanned this large country finally linked up in Utah. Before President Lincoln's assassination, he had pushed through legislation for the Homestead Act, whereby a man could buy 160 acres of land for $1.25 per acre, provided he lived on the land and farmed it for six months. In the next 20 years, millions of settlers passed through Omaha, filing for homesteads on the western prairies. Many of these people were immigrants from Europe, just as I was, seeking freedom from oppression, and hoping for employment or business opportunities.

On December 5, 1870, my wife, Cecelia, presented me with a son, Max Lee. The tobacco shop prospered, and in the ensuing years, we were able to educate the boys, enrolling Max in the Omaha Medical College on Pacific Street.

Max Lee Rich graduated medical school in 1893 and served the communities of Brainard and Wisner before establishing a practice in Grand Island, Nebraska. He served the pioneers and their descendants who settled the plains.

One son, three daughters, two great-granddaughters, and two great-granddaughters-in-law followed in the medical profession.

What a legacy our pioneering forefathers left us. What a privilege to be an American and live the dream that was theirs!

Submitted by Joseph F. Lepant
Grand Island, Nebraska

Yes, We Have No Bananas

My German-born uncle came to the United States during the wave of European immigration in the late 1800s. Though just a small boy, he clearly remembered an incident that happened en route. Someone offered him a banana as a treat. It was the first he'd ever seen, and no one suggested that he peel it first. He tried eating it, peel and all, but it was more than his taste buds could handle. He was a sick boy.

Uncle Alfred grew up, became owner of a successful bakery and married my Aunt Emma. He told her that he never wanted to see a banana—ever again.

Myrna Kautz
Merrill, Wisconsin

Family Made Tough Transition

My mother's family, the Toepfers, lived in Bavaria, Germany. Johann Caspar and his son, Johann, were schoolteachers in the small village of Altenstein from 1778 to 1865. My great-granddad, Johann's son Franz Carl, was a bookbinder in Altenstein. Germany was at war most of the time. Great-Granddad decided to leave Germany because he did not want his sons to serve in the military.

They were members of the Lutheran church. According to church records, the following left for America in 1869: Franz Carl, 48; his second wife, Barbara, 36; Johann, 16; Anna, 11; Christian, 5; and, Heinrich, an infant. This was the beginning of a long journey. I don't know how they got to Bremen, Germany, for embarkation. They boarded the ship *Main*, which took approximately six weeks to arrive in New York on May 31, 1869. The infant boy was not listed as arriving. I can't imagine the hardships they endured. But they were in America, the land of promise and freedom, and so happy.

I believe they traveled by train from New York to Galena, Illinois. Why Franz Carl chose this area I don't know, but it did look a lot like the area in Bavaria where he had lived. In January 1870 he purchased 40 acres of land for $700 in the southeast part of JoDaviess County. Great-Granddad brought gold leaf with him, which he would have used as a bookbinder; this may be what he used for money. We still have one sheet of this gold leaf in our family.

They built their log cabin in the hollow of the hills in order to be near a spring for water. The cabin's foundation is still on the land, which remained in the Toepfer name until recently.

A daughter, Dorothea, was born the following year, and my granddad, Henry, two years later. At the time of Great-Granddad's death in 1883, he had added another 120 acres and built a frame home on high ground; a portion of the house is still there. I always wonder how he was able to adjust to working and living off the land. It would have been rough, hard work compared to bookbinding. It had to be a tough transition.

We thank our great-grandparents for this sacrifice and their decision to leave homeland and family to make a new home in America. All of these immigrants were brave to face the uncertainties of the hard journey ahead of them. How very fortunate we all are to live in a prosperous, free country. May we always be reminded to conserve and maintain what we have so that we can proudly pass on to many generations after us what we received.

Connie Ellis
Farmer City, Illinois

Cow's Milk Made a Meal

On April 18, 1848, Grandpa Helmreich and his bride, four other couples and several other people left Bremerhafen, Germany, on the sail-ship *Regina* for America. Despite unfavorable weather and other disagreeable experiences, they landed in New York on the afternoon of June 3, after being on the ocean three days short of seven weeks. They proceeded on their journey to Bridgeport, then on to Dierkers Barn in Saginaw, where they were met by Pastor Sievers, who came to America in October 1847. The immigrants were to follow him about four weeks later; none of them came to Frankenlust. Some went to Monroe, others to Wisconsin, and some stayed in Frankenmuth.

During the winter, Sievers and a few men from Frankenmuth looked at land by the Tittabawassee River, but found the soil was poor—wet and swampy. Sievers later went 11 miles north of Saginaw on the Squaconning River, where he found what he was looking for and bought 600 acres. He divided it into sections for his people who were to come during the summer of 1848. Wearing high boots and equipped with crude instruments, he tramped through the land to measure off the section, accompanied by hordes of mosquitoes.

At Dierkers Barn the immigrants organized St. Paul's Congregation on June 22, 1848, naming Sievers as their pastor. On June 25 the congregation held its first service with Holy Communion. Sixteen people partook of the Lord's Supper. Four couples were also married that day.

The colonists moved on to their new home in two groups. Some drove the cattle through the forest, with Sievers as their guide. The other group sailed down the Saginaw River on a scow with an attached raft carrying 8,500 feet of lumber, stoves, windows, flour, food, household goods, and most necessary tools, which Andreas Goetz had bought and brought from Detroit for $350. When this group came near the Squaconning River, which was the only way to Frankenlust, they had difficulty getting their scow and raft through the weeds and wild rice, so they did not get there that day. Because they had all the food with them on the scow, the other group did not get anything to eat that evening; only Mr. Hachtel had his meal. He bought one of the best cows, and to be sure she would get to Frankenlust safe and sound, he traveled with the group overland. When it came time to milk the cow, having nothing to milk into, he laid himself under the cow and milked directly into his mouth. He had his meal. The next day the two groups got together again and started to build a shanty. That night it started to rain. It rained for two weeks, so the colonists sat on their boxes and trunks, holding their umbrellas over their heads. A big share of their belongings spoiled, but they all remained in good humor and thanked God that He had led them to a fertile country.

The group going overland heard the sound of cannons being shot in Saginaw, it being the Fourth of July. When they arrived in Frankenlust, they slept the first night under the stars. The place they slept in eventually became a cemetery, where the settlers now rest in peace.

Grace Roedel
Frankenmuth, Michigan

Grandmother Yearned for a Home of Her Own

America—the Land of Opportunity and refuge. "Things will be better if we can only get to America," seems to have been the cry in the 1880s and before.

After my great-grandfather in Germany became ill and died, my great-grandmother, who spoke no English, packed up her mother, her three boys and two girls and moved to America. She had five sisters and two brothers living in Nebraska. Great-Grandmother found employment as a maid with a wealthy family, and she gave her children to her sisters and brothers to raise.

My grandmother, who was 8 years old in 1885, made her home with an aunt. The aunt owned a dry-goods store and had two daughters a little older then my grandmother. The aunt and her family treated Grandmother much like a servant: at 8 years of age, she was responsible for keeping the store spotless. In 1885 there was very little opportunity to travel, even short distances, so Grandmother never saw her mother, even though they were only 50 miles apart. Needless to say my grandmother spent many nights crying of loneliness.

However, there must have been some good in the situation, because by the age of 14 Grandmother could play the piano, knit, embroider, crochet and cook. These facts prove that while the aunt was very demanding of her little German-speaking niece, she also was concerned with teaching her the finer things in life.

Grandmother's loneliness came through when she married at the age of 15. How she must have longed for a home of her own, a place where she truly belonged. Marriage, however, did not bring all sunshine and roses. Grandmother bore 13 children, three of whom died in infancy and another as a young man.

Delores Utecht
Wayne, Nebraska

Almost Buried Too Soon

I have often heard the story of my great-grandparents crossing over. Grandpa was Christoff Meyer, from Trier, Germany. Grandma was Helena Halmos from the old kingdom of Prussia. They were only children at the time. Cholera broke out on the ship, and several died. One of the girls (about 17 years old) was in a coma for several days. Since she showed no sign of life, they believed her dead. They had her laid out on a board to slip her body overboard when her eyes blinked slightly. She got well, later married and raised a family. This story was told and retold many times during our "growing up" years.

Melba Meyer Wiggins
Paden, Oklahoma

Grandfather Brought His Cigar Trade to the States

My great-grandfather, Anton Fangman, was born October 11, 1831, in Leone, Oldenberg, Germany. At 14 he started working in a cigar factory, where he learned the trade.

Later he became a sailor, and for five years sailed to many different countries. At that time German sailors were not allowed to marry. Therefore, after his marriage to Caroline Boeckman on January 10, 1860, they sailed to America.

Anton established a cigar factory in Baltimore, Maryland, where their first son was born. Four years later they moved to Louisville, Kentucky, where he again went into the manufacture of cigars. A daughter was born there.

In 1867, the family traveled by train to St. Charles, Missouri, where they boarded a steamboat bound for Omaha, Nebraska. Anton started the second wholesale and retail cigar manufacturing plant in Omaha. Three more children, including my grandmother, Mary, were born there.

In 1873, they homesteaded 80 acres in Platte County, Nebraska.

Marion Podany
Petersburg, Nebraska

He Winked at "The Lady" and Life

She arrived in America later than my maternal ancestors, but the Statue of Liberty must have meant something to my father, that handsome, debonair, troubled, gifted man who sailed past her into New York Harbor. His people were English and he was the only one of his relatives to come to the United States. Why, I will never know.

There is no longer any record of how my mother's people came. There is only a legend about one of them. A man, whose surname was Swisher, came from Germany and took an unusual route to becoming an American. Judging by the Swishers I knew, he must have been short of stature, ready for adventure and not about to die of hunger. There were fearful shortages of food all over Europe in the late 1700s, and there were few advancement chances for young men.

When the English recruiter came to Hesse, the legend goes, this Swisher signed up to fight for the British in their colonial war against the upstart American rebels. We can only imagine his good-byes to all his relatives and his last looks at his town or family farm as he left all that he knew. We can imagine his short training, the voyage over the Atlantic and how he must have felt to be on dry land in the New World.

We can only imagine his impressions of life in this Land of Opportunity, how he first began to dream his larger dream, when he first knew battle, and how and when he prayed.

We can be nearly certain that he was at Trenton, New Jersey, on Christmas night, 1776, when Washington crossed the Delaware River. We can also assume that he was involved in the battle the next day, for the Hessians did the fighting there for the English; of course, they were defeated by Washington's cold and hungry forces.

We descendants know he survived the battle because we are here. He faded into the forest of this new country, and his son—or grandson—took a Conestoga wagon west to Ohio. There the family settled at Mogador, which no longer exists. My grandfather, Milton Euclydus Swisher, told me his grandfather went to visit his father at St. Johns, Indiana, which is also non-existent now, but was near Auburn, Indiana. He died there and had the dubious distinction of being the first white person to be buried in the old cemetery near present-day downtown Auburn.

The Swishers were almost all farmers—those who stayed nearby. Others drifted on to Montana and Texas. Most were great workers and owned many acres for that time.

On my maternal grandmother's side, all were of English stock, and there were many pioneer spirits among them. One I like to think of is her maternal grandfather, the Rev. Josiah Shugars, a circuit riding Presbyterian minister from Cairo, Illinois. He rode horseback many miles to conduct church services and Christian rites. He was also a carpenter. I have a butterfly table that he made of cherry wood and two picture frames that he carved.

Some years ago I circled the Statue of Liberty in a tourist boat, marveling at the statue and all that it has meant and means now to so many people. I couldn't help but be happy that some of my ancestors braved the elements—and maybe their families—to come to America.

When I was a young anyone-can-cover-everything reporter, I covered a speech by a stirring orator who talked about these people who dared so much. His key phrase was: "And only the brave came!" It was an awakening experience to hear him, for life then was very safe and orderly in the Midwest. He went on to tell us that those brave people who came had their horizons widened by the vastness of the land before it was settled. That unknown orator and the Statue have given me much to think about.

My father did see The Lady. He was a failure in England. Apprenticed to a printer, he failed. As a soldier in the British Army in Egypt, he was thought to have been "bought out." He was given passage money to America, where he promptly made it to San Francisco in time for the great earthquake. He did some high-wire work and had his own medicine show—traveling, that is.

If the high hopes he felt when he first saw The Lady never materialized, he was seldom bored; England could not have offered him what the new land did. A columnist for 17 years, a radio personality for 11, owner of a repertoire company, a clown with Barnum and Bailey—he did all of this and found at least 20 other ways to pass the time. I'm sure he was glad he came.

Father, the son of a Chester, England, silk merchant, passed the Lady three times. The second and third time he was with his first wife, a blonde Cuban. They were hired as entertainers for a large ocean liner. They visited his relatives in England and returned.

At that time they were adagio dancers. She died in childbirth shortly thereafter.

I know he didn't realize all his dreams—no one does. He wanted to act on Broadway. He started in early movies, with a bit part in one of the "Perils of Pauline" series, but that was the high point of his movie involvement.

Years after he died, his only daughter, her husband and six grandchildren would see and admire The Lady, circling her in a small craft. Traces of Ritchie—or Rube, or Hokus-Pokus, but really Harold Charles—could be seen in their vague resemblance to him, as well as in their theatrical use of six mother-and-daughter blue-on-white polka dot dresses.

Yes, The Lady could not have failed to interest him.

Knowing him I wonder: Did he wink at The Lady as he passed by her?

After all, he winked at life.

> Betty Brown Hicks
> Eufaula, Alabama

A Letter from my Grandmother

Well, Gloria, you want me to tell you something about my trip over the ocean. Well, there is not much to tell, you know I was only 13, and children don't think much. They take things the way they come.

We left Germany the first of March, 1868. We were put on the ship in the afternoon, and the steamer lifted anchor right away before we were settled in our bunk. When we went on deck, we could see no land any more, but we were not on the Atlantic Ocean but in the North Sea. But the Sea was as smooth and as calm as a floor.

There were 900 people on board, and all were afraid to get Sea sick. They told everybody to walk against the wind, then we would not get Sea sick. So everybody tried it and you ought to have seen the people walk. But before long a Russian stepped to the rail and vomited, you know that is the Sea sickness, and everybody laughed at him. But it didn't take long—one after another did the same thing, and I did too.

So soon the deck was empty. They all were too sick to stay up. Next morning we were at Liverpool, England. There we stopped 24 hours and took in provisions, and you ought to have seen the stuff people brought on board—whole halves of beef and boatloads of vegetables. If anybody wanted to go on shore, the sailors would take them.

Well, next day we went on our trip to America. There were larger waves than in the North Sea. Sometimes we could see ships in the distance riding on a high wave. Then all at once it was gone, and a large wave came between that ship and the one we were on.

It was quite interesting to sit and watch the waves and the people. Some were laughing, some were crying (they were homesick already.) Some were singing, some played the accordion, some the French harp. Then some were dancing, so you see it was not lonesome, and we were feeling good after the first three day were over (the Sea sickness lasted three days—but mother was sick from the first day to the last.)

We had better eating than we were use to, but we had to go to the kitchen to get it. And we had no table to eat at. Each one took their plate on their lap. We got supper in a bucket, vegetables and meat in a pan, and pudding in another pan (all the dishes were of tin so they would not break.) And we had to get our own dishes and our own bedding before we left Hamburg (Germany). That was in the contract.

Well, the first week went on alright, but then one day men came down with ropes and tied the trunks to the bunks. Someone asked why they did that and they said the trunks slide and someone get hurt. But other men came and screwed heavy iron caps over the little round windows and lighted up the lanterns.

Then they were asked what was up. Oh, they said, nothing much, only we expect a pocketful of wind tonight. It sure was more than a pocketful. The wind began to howl something fierce. And the ship rolled from one side to the other.

Sometimes it felt as if it stood on its head, sometimes on its tail end. It *was terrible. Some of the women screamed, some prayed, some moaned. No one slept. It was enough to make a person crazy.*

That kept on for three days, but at last people quieted down. They got used to it. No one could go on deck. The doors were fastened. Only a small place over the doors was left open for fresh air.

I was smart and went up to take a look and got a spray of rain on my head. A man told me to go down before I got all wet. Well, I did but came almost down head first. The storm tore away some of the banister and did some other damage.

When the storm was over, the men fixed up the damage, and we could go on deck again. It was nice weather till we came to America.

The day before we landed the pilot came in a small boat to pilot us into the harbor. The ship stopped not far from an island, I think it was Staten Island, where they guaranteed people. The doctors came on board, and we were all examined.

Then we went on to the harbor, where we were unloaded and all the trunks and boxes opened and examined. Then they took us to a large round building (it is not standing any more), where they kept us for three days till an immigrant train was ready to take people further in the country.

Immigrant trains were not so expensive as the regular passenger trains, but the immigrant trains were so slow that it took us over a week to get from New York to Hannibal and we almost died for some sleep.

Well, I could see no difference between here and Germany. Only we couldn't understand people. But there were German people everywhere to help us along. Most of the train men spoke German.

Well, it took me two days to write this down. I guess you could have done it in a few hours. Ships are larger now. They won't roll like the one we came over in. The price was $50 for storage, $100 for cabin.

Grandma Frank
Submitted by
Glorietta Rhody King
Louisiana, Missouri

Travelers Saw Chicago Fire Damage Firsthand

My great-grandfather, Joseph A. Roth Sr., was the son of a prominent family in Wertenburg, Germany. He studied extensively, spoke seven languages, and was completing preparation for the Divinity when he abruptly left Germany. A stowaway, he paid for his passage to the United States by working in a ship's galley. He first settled in Illinois, where he married. They left Illinois for LeMars, Iowa, by train. When they came through the Chicago area, the train was side-tracked because of the big fire that had just occurred. From the train they could see the devastation the fire had left. When they arrived in LeMars, an old friend met them.

Great-Grandpa Roth erected a sod hut on his land claim, but Great-Grandma's health could not take the dampness. They stayed with friends until a 14-by-16 log cabin was built.

The first years they used oxen for hauling logs, for field work, and for transportation.

Grasshoppers plagued them for about seven years. During these times Great-Grandpa Roth taught school and broke sod for other settlers. In this way he was able to earn enough money to provide for his family. He also held German classes for merchants, so they could communicate with the many German settlers who were beginning to come to northwest Iowa.

Myrtle May Duin
George, Iowa

Light-Hearted Dad Made Life Fun

My father was born in Husun, Schleswig-Holstein, Germany, in 1887. In 1904, at the age of 17, he came to America. His passage was paid by a farmer near Atlantic, Iowa, in exchange for farm labor. He traveled with a friend, sailed the ocean, came through the emigrant station at Ellis Island, and traveled by train to Iowa. My dad and his friend got separated while boarding the train and ended up in separate train cars. His friend had the good fortune of having their lunch in his possession. Daddy got very hungry before realizing that one could pass from one train car to the next. He was also introduced to his first tomato on this trip. Thinking them to be apples, he bought one. One bite assured him that this apple was rotten, and he threw it away!

He worked hard to earn passage for his brother and two sisters, leaving three brothers in Germany. My father Americanized his name to William Frederick Molck. When he realized that he could not maneuver in Iowa soil in his clogs, he simply discarded them for more American-type shoes. He taught himself to read, write and speak English. He was awarded his citizenship papers in 1939 at the age of 52. He started our Christmas morning tradition of singing "Silent Night": we in English, Daddy in German.

Though he died when I was only 8, I learned from him that Germans are hard-working, fun-loving people. Daddy would sing and shodish around our home when he was in a light-hearted mood (which was often). His heart was as big as he was, and he taught my Scotch mother to offer callers hospitality, even if it was the last crumb of bread in the house!

Vicki L. (Molck) Christensen
Anita, Iowa

Son Helped Family Realize Father's Dream

My great-grandparents, Paul and Augusta, sailed on *The Deutcha Vandaha* to the United States in 1881. Before they came this family of 11 sold all their possessions except what they needed for daily use. The money helped pay for the ship's passage. Their 23-year-old son, Carl, had gone to the States several years earlier because he feared being drafted in the German army. He made his way to the Midwest by doing odd jobs until he reached Omaha, Nebraska. He found a good job in a butcher shop there. He wrote to his family to come to the States, which is why Great-Grandfather and his family set sail for America.

All went well on the journey. They arrived in Omaha in the spring of 1881. Great-Grandfather found a home for his family and a good job. But four months later tragedy fell upon the family. Great-Grandfather became violently ill and died August 17, 1881. What was a young mother to do? The oldest girl was able to do housework that was much in demand in those days. The teenage boys did small jobs about the city. Carl had applied for a homestead in northeast Nebraska and soon he proved up 160 acres of land. Carl saved enough money from his butchering job to buy a team of horses and a lumber wagon, a walking plow, some tools and other supplies. With these supplies and some of his brothers, he left Omaha for the homestead. The land was primitive, so Carl had to live under the wooden box of his wagon. Wild animals were always around, sometimes to be feared and sometimes to be eaten. When he got a house built it served as a shelter for his horses, too.

When summer came and school was out, Great-Grandmother took her small children and traveled to Carl's homestead to help him out and plant a big garden of potatoes and other vegetables. She spent many summer days canning and preserving the good things from the garden so they would have plenty of food through the winter months when they lived in Omaha. Great-Grandmother's children grew up to be fine citizens of this country, through very hard work, many sacrifices and their strong Lutheran faith. Great-Grandmother lived to be 92.

Caroline Abendroth Zuhlke
Bancroft, Nebraska

Great Depression Took Its Toll on Immigrants, Too

Both sets of my grandparents emigrated from different parts of Germany during the last decades of the 1800s. They came at different times; my paternal ones came from the area called Mecklenburg; the maternal two came from the Hessian state. All probably used the steerage part of their ship. Their destination was America's Midwest; they probably came through the country by train.

The four all settled in northeast Iowa, about 12 miles apart: Grandfather Dohrmann near Tripoli, Iowa; my maternal Grandfather Judas near the small town of Readlyn.

My dad's father bought 160 acres near Tripoli. He lost his young, first wife through death; she left two small children. A few years later he married a young German lady from Mecklenburg. I recently learned that she was probably sponsored by Grandpa's neighbor, who helped bring over young German women to become the brides of lonely immigrant men. Five children were born to this new marriage—one was my father. Death came easily in those times—two of the children died early in life.

The 160 acres my Grandfather Dohrmann bought was considered a big place at that time. I grew up on those acres when my parents rented the place after Grandpa and Grandma moved to town, and I knew every nook and cranny of those fields. When my paternal grandparents moved to town, we drifted into The Depression, and an insurance company where my grandparents had borrowed money took over all but 40 acres of the land. We had no idea that times were so difficult for them. My parents bought the remaining 40 acres and lived there until they moved to town.

Grandfather was a studious man, with a small library of impressive books written in German. He was always reading. He was aloof and couldn't easily talk to his grandchildren. My grandmother was talkative and friendly, but I had to be careful about what I said and asked—Grandma could cut with the edge of her tongue.

My mother's parents fared much better. They bought a farm near Readlyn, had a nice house in town when they retired and left their children a sizeable inheritance. I loved my maternal grandmother, she was kind and considerate. Although I was only 4, I remember the night she died—all the family was outside on the lawn while the mortician was in the house. I fell asleep in Grandmother's flower bed.

For me the difference in the German dialects was both funny and serious at times. My father thought my mother's Hessian plat-deutch was wrong and his Mecklenburger dialect was right, and he often laughed at her different words. To avoid being laughed at, my sister and I chose Dad's way of speaking German.

Lucinda Boeckmann
Tripoli, Iowa

Good Fortune a Gift from Ancestors

My ancestors, all of whom emigrated from areas of northern Germany prior to the Civil War, must have been driven by adventure, ambition and dreams of creating a better life for themselves, as well as for their descendants. This they did, in spite of the hardships and adversities they encountered in wrestling a productive life from what was a rather hostile wilderness.

In my memory remain vague references to their long, unpleasant voyage across the rough North Atlantic and the difficulties and indignities suffered during their processing through Ellis Island. Following the rail trip from New York City to Chicago they were faced with an austere, frontier way of life. After a few years of struggling for a foothold, the appeal of obtaining land of their own in then-distant Iowa possessed them. My paternal grandfather, a lad of about 14, took on the task of making the initial move. He hired on as a hand to assist an immigrant group on their way to Iowa, caring for their stock along the way. He somehow managed to duly file a homestead claim before returning to Illinois. That next spring found him and his parents in another immigrant group, on their way toward establishing themselves upon the land that he had claimed the year before.

The ensuing privations, disappointments and hard work can only be imagined. Establish themselves they did, as did their neighbors. Not only did they achieve their personal goals; collectively they also founded places for worshipping and obtaining basic education for all in the region. They also supported and nourished the beginnings of small nearby communities.

It was not all adventure. There was illness and death. Work and privation tested the soul. The heat of summer and the bitter cold of winter seemed unbearable. Storms and pestilence vexed them. Through all of this, they persevered. Most of them lived to enjoy some of the blessings of their labors.

The enormity of the task that lay before them upon their arrival was best displayed for me one beautiful, clear October day. I was enjoying the comfort of an airliner, streaking high above a portion of my boyhood world. Spread out below were the lands where my ancestors and myriad others had devoted their lives toward the creation of a better life. As I viewed this "New Land" the thought struck me; surely there were those who deplored the transformation of wild lands into developed, productive countryside. But I staunchly subscribe to the precept that humankinds' mission is to accept the bounties of nature and convert them into what best serves all of humanity.

Who among us can measure up to the trials, adversities, heartaches and labors that our forebears endured? In most cases, the blessings were not theirs to savor. We, their descendants, have reaped the full measure of their labors. All too often, we do not fully appreciate our good fortune. Nor do we afford them full credit for the comfortable lifestyles that we lead, for which they labored so diligently.

These were our ancestors: great-grandparents, grandparents and parents. May all of us pay greater homage to these wonderful, heroic, indomitable people who created the potential for our way of life and gave us so much to be thankful for.

The indomitable people who were instrumental in the transformation of the lands constituting the United States of America are to be venerated. They gave us a legacy that is second to none.

Homer Nevermann
Seattle, Washington

Winds of War Sent Family to America

I was born in 1938 in a small Bavarian village in Germany before the Second World War. It was a very cold winter with lots of snow. I was too small to remember, but the winds of war were in the making. My father and brother were called to serve their country. It was a very unhappy time in my homeland. Many countries were at war, and people's lives and countries were destroyed. Peace came in the spring of 1945. Seven years went by before my father and brother came home again. We all went to church and sang God's praises again and again.

In 1949 my oldest brother left for the United States. He was born there in 1925, for my mom and dad had lived in the States from 1923 to 1929 before returning to Bavaria to find work. In 1954, my family of eight went back to the United States. It was a very happy day when my brother picked us up from the boat after a very long trip on the stormy seas. I was seasick for 11 days and lost 10 pounds. So glad we were to put our feet on land again. New Jersey was our first address, and we still live there today. We all found work; I was a nanny for two small children at the shore. We all went to school at night and worked during the day.

At 21 I got married. We have a son and a daughter. They are the first in our family to graduate from a university, and they hold top positions in Manhattan, New York. America—the beautiful Land of Opportunity.

Theresa M. Herzig
Towaco, New Jersey

Family Settled in the Wilds of Nebraska

My grandparents did indeed come from the old country, or old countries. My father's parents came from Germany, and even now I have relatives there whom I have never had the pleasure of hearing from. However, one of my cousins and his wife lived in Germany for a little more than two years and became acquainted with some of our relatives. It was his privilege to bring back a picture of our grandfather when he was a young man, made from a newspaper picture.

My father's name was Fey, and his father, John N. Fey, and his mother, Augusta Fischer, both emigrated from Germany.

When I was a very small child my grandmother went back to Germany to see her family. She had brothers there. They wanted her to make her home in Germany, so they persuaded her to marry while there. Her first husband had died when my father, the oldest of their children, was 16. She did marry again while in Germany, but not with the intention of staying there. Her new husband had asthma and was not allowed to sail on the ship, so she came back to the States alone and got a divorce.

My mother's family name was Newcomer after they arrived in the United States from Switzerland. The clerk could not spell their name so just put it down as Newcomer. They left Germany because of religious persecution.

Some of the Newcomer relatives settled in parts of Nebraska where only Indians and a few settlers lived. One of Mother's relatives was Rev. James Query, the first preacher in that area. He and his family had some interesting experiences with Indians. The Newcomer family grew to include Uncle Frank Hibbler, who lived in a log house. There was also an Uncle Tom Record. They were my mother's great-uncles.

One of her great-uncles came to visit us on the farm in Nebraska. He enjoyed sitting in a rocking chair on the front porch, which faced the road. He had a saying that I still remember—"Yes sir, you know sir, it's a nice day today," regardless of the weather. Mother made some marmalade while he was there. I remember it because he enjoyed it a great deal, while the rest of the family did not care for it.

My mother's mother was Alice Davis. I have no information about her. She died when my mother was 3 years old. Her father was Frank Newcomer. He later married a widow with children. They moved to western Oklahoma by covered wagon.

They settled 40 miles from the nearest town, where they could buy things like flour, sugar, etc. Grandpa had to go by wagon. It was necessary to go through an Indian encampment. The Indians were friendly and always asked Grandpa to stop for a meal. He graciously declined each time. He was afraid they might serve dog meat.

When cotton was ready to pick, the children were taken out of school to pick—first at home, then for the neighbors. Life was hard. The Newcomer grandparents asked that my mother come stay with them so that her grandmother could make her a new dress. When the dress was finished they did not let her go back to her folks; life then was easier for her.

Hazel Houston
Huxley, Iowa

Grandfather Transplanted Farming Skills to America

Grandpa Philipp was born in Horrenberg, Germany, on March 30, 1876. His father was Wendelen and his mother was Theresa. The children were Rose, Bertha, Carl, Frank, and Eugene, the youngest. Horrenberg was a little country village near Heidelberg. Grandpa grew up on a farm and helped with the horses, cattle and sheep. Rose married and came to America, as her husband was to accompany his sister. Their brother was a priest in America and wanted the sister to be his housekeeper.

In America, Rose lived on a farm four miles north of Ellinwood, Kansas. She was homesick for some of her family. Grandpa's older brothers didn't want to come to America as they both had girl-friends in Germany. Later, Frank had to go into the army. Because of a broken jawbone, Carl was not eligible for service. Eugene, our grandfather, wanted to come to America, but his father thought he was too young to leave home. They later learned that Mr. Creulich was coming to America to visit a son who was a priest. Grandpa's father then consented for him to come with Mr. Creulich.

On July 30, 1892, at the age of 16, Grandpa left Germany for America. There were approximately 1,600 people on the ship *Spardum*. After a 12-day voyage, they arrived in America on a hot August day. Grandpa didn't have much to say about the ship ride to America. He recalls that the ladies stayed on one side of the ship and the men on the other. The men had fun teasing the ladies about being sick. Grandpa said most everyone got sick, including him.

The people aboard the ship were taken to Castle Garden in New York, where they had to wait for trains to take them on their way. Grandpa and Mr. Creulich traveled together as far as Chicago by train. Grandpa recalled Mr. Creulich telling him to go to sleep and when he woke up Mr. Creulich would be gone. When Grandpa awoke, sure enough, he was gone. Grandpa never saw him again, although Grandpa did learn through correspondence that Mr. Creulich lived with his son in Louisville, Kentucky, for some time and later moved to Michigan to be with his sister. Grandpa was on his own.

In spite of his youth, he didn't encounter any major problems while finding his way to Ellinwood, Kansas. His father had told him to send his sister a telegram when he arrived in America so she would know that he was coming to see her, but Grandpa, a stranger to his new surroundings, completely forgot about it. He traveled by train to Kansas. Although he couldn't speak any English, he got along real well. He knew that priest Simon Epp, his brother-in-law's brother at Ellinwood, Kansas, would help him find Rose and Simon. Grandpa recalled that the train came into Ellinwood from the east.

When he got off the train, he met a lady walking toward him on the street. He asked her the way to the priest's house. She couldn't speak German, but she motioned with her hands to give directions. Grandpa walked a short way and soon noticed a church with a cross on the steeple. When he got to the church he recognized the hymns, which were being sung in German. He stood in the back of the church until the service was over. As people were leaving he asked a lady where the priest's house was. She spoke to him and very kindly took him there with her. She was the priest's housekeeper and a sister of Grandpa's brother in-law, so she knew who Grandpa was.

Soon the priest came home. He said Grandpa should spend the night with them and he would help him meet Rose and Simon in the morning. The next day was Sunday, and the priest was to offer Mass at the country settlement where Rose and her family attended. It was named St. Peter & Paul. Grandpa went with the priest and met his sister Rose there.

Grandpa recalled she was very happy to see him. He lived with his sister and her family for four years. He felt at home there because of the children and her farm animals. He attended a country school the first winter he lived in America. He had attended high school in Germany but he wanted to learn English, which he did. He also helped his brother-in-law. About this time, the Cherokee Strip was opened for settlement in Oklahoma. Anyone at least 21 years old was eligible to stake 160 acres of land free. They were to build a shanty and drill a water well on it. Grandpa wasn't eligible to stake a claim because of his age, but he went on the run with his friends from Barton County and helped them stake their claims.

Grandpa wanted to take up farming for his own, so he used the $476 that his father had given him when he left home to buy his land in Oklahoma. He had also worked for $8 a month the first year and $12 a month the second year, saving this money to use when he decided to start out on his own. Grandpa also worked on the railroad whenever he could and on a threshing crew, where he earned $1.25 a day or about $60 a season. Grandpa was proud to have a farm of his own, as this was his first farming experience where he was boss. He had a horse, which his sister had given him, but he had to buy work horses and a plow. He also bought a brand new wagon for $55. He built a shanty on his land.

His first major problem occurred when he drilled a well for water on his land. Everyone in the area was making their wells just 20 feet deep, so Grandpa did too. He contracted typhoid fever from the water and was taken to the hospital in Wichita. Grandpa said he was fortunate to be released from the hospital after a two-month stay, as many people died with typhoid fever that year. Rose had him stay with her until he was stronger, then he returned to his own farm. He then drilled his well 50 feet deep, and he didn't have any more trouble with it.

Grandpa said he usually rode the freight trains for his trips to Ellinwood to visit Rose and his friends, the Arons brothers. About three years after he moved to Oklahoma, Rose and her family did too. Grandpa recalls that the first two years were poor ones and no crops were harvested. Many people left the area during this time. The third year was better, and soon the settlement progressed. Many people built new homes. A Catholic church 30 feet wide and 50 feet long was also built. It was a frame building. Grandpa was chosen to haul the sand for this project because he had a new wagon that wouldn't break down. He hauled the first load of sand for the church, which they named St. Peter and Paul. This church was named after the church that they had attended in Barton County, Kansas.

The priest in charge of this church came only once a month, and he couldn't speak any German. The people were unhappy about this so they reported it to the bishop. This priest was replaced by a priest from Belgium who could speak German, but it wasn't his native tongue, so he spoke English instead. Rose and her family didn't speak English at all and felt that their religious needs weren't being met. They decided to find a settlement that had a German priest, so they put an ad in a newspaper. They were pleased to receive a letter from a man in Charleston, Arkansas, who said that they had a German settlement there with plenty of farmland. Simon and Rose decided to move their family to this German settlement in Arkansas.

Grandpa remained in Oklahoma, but he went to visit his sister in Arkansas for Christmas. Valentine Gilsinger was a neighbor of Rose's who had several daughters, one named Elizabeth. Grandpa met the Gilsingers during his visit, and he and Elizabeth corresponded when he returned to Oklahoma. They were married at the Sacred Heart Catholic Church in Charleston, Arkansas, on February 14, 1905. Grandpa sold his farm in Oklahoma in 1905 for $3,000. He bought a farm in Arkansas for $1,900. He built a house and other buildings on it and erected his first wire fences. This was an improvement from the wooden fences, which the cattle easily broke.

Grandpa raised cotton on this farm. Since he used the barn manure to fertilize his fields, he had big bales of cotton to sell. He had learned to do this in Germany. He hand-picked his cotton crop. Three of Grandpa and Grandma's children were born while they were living in Arkansas: Lenora, January 1906; Carl, April 1907; and Rose, September 1908. In November of 1908, they decided to leave Arkansas because Grandpa didn't like cotton farming. He was used to wheat farming, and the cotton farm was just too different for him.

Grandpa read an ad in the German newspaper *Ladman* about a man in Ellis county who wanted to trade for a farm in Arkansas. They traded farms, and Grandpa and Grandma moved to their new 160 acre farm 1 mile west and 2 miles north of Ellis, Kansas. Another daughter, Margaret, was born in November of 1913. While they lived on this farm Grandpa raised wheat, horses, cattle and chickens. He also had a job as a rural mail carrier. Carl and Lenora attended St. Marys School in Ellis.

In 1914, Grandpa and Grandma decided to move to Durant, Oklahoma. They moved all of their farm animals, machinery, and household furniture and goods to Oklahoma in a boxcar on the freight train. After six months there, they didn't like the climate and country so they moved back to their Ellis County farm, of which they still had possession. When this farm was sold, Grandpa bought a 320 acre farm for $8,000 in Trego county, five and one-half miles southwest of Ellis. They moved to it in August 1915.

Grandpa built onto this house, adding a new barn and granary and a shed for his buggies. He said he had a hard time getting started in Kansas. They sold cream and eggs and worked hard farming the land. The children attended St. Mary's School in Ellis and later attended South Glenco School in Trego County, which was one-half mile west of their home. This was Grandpa's last farm and he loved it dearly. All of his grandchildren can recall the stories he loved to share while walking through the pasture to bring the cows home to milk. Margaret and her husband, Frank Schneller, now own Grandpa's farm. Grandpa and Grandma Philipp moved to Ellis, Kansas, in 1955. Grandma passed away on January 23, 1967, at the age of 82. Grandpa passed away on September 27, 1971, at the age of 95.

Ellen Farrell
Hill City, Kansas

Boys Bravely Defended Cornfield

My husband's grandparents left Doelitz, Pomerania, Germany, April 11, 1866. Their family consisted of four boys, ages 12 to 3, and a baby girl, age 4 months. With nearly all the money they had in the world spent for the cheapest passage, this family started on the long voyage to America on the ship, *Eugenie*, with Captain Cahnbley in charge. Their personal effects were very few, and their only food those several weeks on the sea was the bread and crackers they had made before leaving Germany. On a sea voyage, bread that old takes on strange tastes, odors and colors.

It is not likely that the children's mother sang "Rock a Bye Baby," as a lullaby on the journey, for the voyage was very rough. Waves of mountainous proportions swept entirely over the boat, and even though the hatches were closed, considerable amounts of ocean water found its way to the holds of their steerage passage. It took them almost three months to make the journey. Seven weeks of this time they were afloat on the ocean in a sailboat—in those days steamboats were few and seldom used by the poorer classes. They landed at the Port of Immigration Station at New York about June 6.

Great disappointment was this immigrant family's first re-action on arrival in America, for the baby girl, who had smallpox, was placed in quarantine on Castle Clinton, later known as Ellis Island. They immediately learned the hard way that this nation safeguarded the lives and health of its citizens. The mother and babe were taken to a hospital and quarantined, and the father waited for their release.

Money—what was it? Something they had very very little of, so the family separated. The four little boys, with no money in their pockets and their fares paid in advance, were compelled to continue their journey with an uncle and his family to the "extreme west," as it was called at that time: the land of Indians, buffalo and deer.

They came as far as St. Joseph, Missouri, by rail, which took a week, then traveled two days on a steamboat, which was more to their liking, up the Missouri River as far as Brownville, Nebraska. They then traveled by oxen team to Muddy Creek in Johnson County, near Auburn, where they stayed two weeks while waiting for the boys' parents to join them. The baby died in New York. Reportedly the mother later sent money to a New York nunnery to repay it for taking care of her and arranging the burial. The family then continued on to Jefferson County, Nebraska, arriving at their homestead just in time to spend their first Fourth of July in America.

During that first year, 20 acres were broken and planted with corn and pumpkins. They were very hungry, and they worked long and prayed for a crop. Being very poor was not a sin, but to stay poverty stricken would have been unthinkable to the pioneers, for they were healthy and industrious. They measured their stride against hardships, anxiety, droughts and disappointments and won. If one was to eat, he had to work; this law of self-preservation applied to men, women and children alike.

In their new home, the family experienced a thrilling incident with the Indians. The early settlers were extremely alarmed when a report came that wild Indians, the Sioux, had captured two children, a girl and a boy, about 20 miles away. The Sioux and another tribe were warring between each other, and the girl was exchanged for other war prisoners. When the second tribe later traveled through her territory, the girl found her way home. She reported that the Indians had killed her brother, who was the younger of the two, on account of him crying so much and being homesick.

This report caused great alarm. As Great-Grandfather had no team at this time, he walked about six miles and borrowed one. They loaded their few belongings, and, taking two cows and two pigs, went back to where the neighbors were fortifying. This was in August. The stock had to walk this six miles, and the pigs died of heat on the way.

My great-grandfather had 20 acres of sod corn, which looked very good. This was their only outlook for support. A neighbor two miles from this cornfield owned quite a herd of cattle, and as there were no fences or herd laws and everything roamed at will, that cornfield had to be protected.

My great-grandfather was employed mowing wild hay with a scythe for others, so it fell to the lot of two little boys, 10 and 8 years old, to guard this cornfield. Barefoot, they traveled the six miles each way each day for about a week. Then, getting bolder, they took eats along to last more than one day. A dog was their only companion. One nice morning the boys overslept. The dog, making a great noise, awakened them. Thinking that there was something wrong outside, one boy looked out from the door of the dugout and spied the Indians sneaking along the side of the creek. To say that he was frightened would be putting it mildly. A hasty consultation took place between the two boys. Their first plan was to strike direct to the homefolks, six miles away, but looking in their starting direction, an Indian was right in their path. Thinking of a neighbor who might be home, they made a hasty retreat in the opposite direction. They were much relieved to find him there. Telling him of the Indians they had seen, he doubted them at first, saying, "Oh, you boys are scared." Seeing that they were determined in their belief, he said, "Let's go over to my watermelon patch across the creek and prove it," as he was certain the Indians would be after watermelons if near. They accompanied him to the melon patch, where four or five husky fellows were slashing melons right and left.

In the neighbor's former experiences with the Indians, he had learned a few words. Soon he began doing business with them, swapping his melons for such things as they carried: a bridle, a butcher knife, etc. Of course it turned out to be only a scare—they were a friendly tribe—but it might have been real.

Ruby Zabel
Daykin, Nebraska

—■—

Chapter Four: The Eastern European Connection

Sod Houses and Centipedes

Jacob H. Boehs was born in the village Antanofka, Poland Russia, in 1858. At the age of 14 he lost his father. His mother remarried one year later. That same year, on December 4, 1874, he left his homeland with his parents, brothers and sisters. They embarked with 710 other passengers on the *SS Vaterland.* Sailing wasn't smooth; they encountered violent storms. They lost all three propeller blades en route across the Atlantic. They arrived in Philadelphia on December 25, 1874.

Great-Grandfather William took sick while on ship. Prayers were said, asking that he be spared till they reached America so they wouldn't need to bury him at sea. He died several days after they reached land.

On December 27, 1874, they left for Kansas by train, arriving on the 30th. It was a cold winter day, 12 below zero. They spent their first winter in Florence, Kansas. Living quarters were poor, and the death rate amongst them was high. A child reportedly died every other night. Jacob's parents later moved to Durham, Kansas, where they made their home.

Jacob spent three years working in Illinois, where he learned English. Wages were low: the first year they were $8 a month; the second year, $10 a month; the third year, $12 a month.

At 26 he married Susanna Koehn of Durham, Kansas. Their first nine and one-half years together were spent in Kansas. Henry,

John, Ben, Helena, Solomon, Anna, Jacob and Sam were born there; Solomon and Jacob died in infancy.

Jacob became interested in Oklahoma when he heard about staking a claim for free land. He purchased a fast black horse and trained him. He wanted to be sure he wasn't among the slow ones making the run. He staked his claim south of Caldwell, Oklahoma. It wasn't long until a big black man showed up with a gun. He said, "This is my claim." So Jacob gave it up and returned to his family in Durham.

In December of that same year, he, with Henry Nightengale and Adam Jantz, went by wagon to the Fairview vicinity to look for free land. He staked his claim December 1, 1893. The 160 acres were in tall native grass. He then returned to his family.

In March 1894 the Boehs packed up their belongings: a wagon, three horses, two cows, one tom turkey, a few chickens and some seed potatoes. They rented a train car to Enid, Oklahoma. From there they went by wagon to their homestead farm.

When they arrived at the Cimarron River, their hopes were shattered. The land before them was a desolate scene. It had been blackened by a prairie fire. The shanty of two-by-fours that Jacob had built was destroyed. He had a look at the soil. Taking a handful of it, he asked in German, "Will I make it here?" They found another old shack to move into till he could make a dugout. The first summer they planted potatoes and broomcorn in the burnt soil. The broomcorn crop netted $80, which wouldn't go far with a large, growing family. The crops that were sold were taken to Enid by horse and wagon. Crossing the Cimarron River wasn't all that easy, either. If the water was up, it meant waiting several hours before crossing.

They spent their first winter in the dugout, with $8 to carry them through till spring. The following spring, with the help of neighbors, Jacob built a sod house, which took only a week. Those sod houses were no mansions. Snakes and centipedes were plentiful. Once Jacob was finishing his cup of coffee when he noticed a large centipede in the bottom of his cup. Sometimes skunks got in the house too.

During their first years of pioneering in Oklahoma, Lizzie, Susie and Mary were born. In February 1902, Susie's dress caught fire. She received extensive burns and passed away that evening; she was nearly 3 years old.

Once when Jacob was in need of a pair of shoes and he had no money, he went to town and asked the storekeeper if he could mortgage his team of horses for a pair of shoes. The storekeeper replied he couldn't put a team of horses in his register. So Jacob returned home, wrapped his feet in burlap and went to the field.

On February 21, 1904, Jacob lost his beloved Susanna, six weeks after giving birth to a stillborn child.

March 21, 1905, Jacob married Anna Koehn, Susanna's cousin. Anna took over the responsibilities of a large family. To this union Pete, Dena, Ida, Lydia and Martha were born. Tragedy came again to their home. Little Dena, 1-and-one-half-years old, found a cork with fly poison on the window sill. She died the same evening, June 24, 1907.

Jacob never owned a tractor. His farming was all done by horses. He built a barn in 1913 that withstood many storms and still stands today, with a slight slant. The big, open hayloft was sometimes used as a social gathering place. He had one pony and 12 horses for field work. Jacob died January 2, 1942; Anna, September 22, 1963.

Esther Schmidt
Moundridge, Kansas

Homestead Stays in the Family

In March 1872 my grandfather got a passport for him, his wife and son, John, to come to the United States from Prague. His wife never reached the United States; whether she died or never boarded no one knows. They landed and went to Cleveland, Ohio, where more people from the old country had settled.

In 1873 my grandfather remarried, this time to a woman whose parents had gone west to Iowa. Grandfather asked the owners of the land adjacent to his in-laws' acreage whether they would sell it. The landowners, who lived in Cleveland, asked $200 for the 40 acres; Grandma said to offer $180. If the offer was accepted they would have $20 to buy a cow.

The owners accepted the $180. My grandparents put all their possessions in two trunks, one of which my grandfather made before coming to the United States that is still in use today. They boarded the train and came to Fonda, Iowa.

Leaving their trunks at the depot, they walked across the prairie to Grandma's parents. Then Grandpa borrowed a team of horses and drove back to Fonda to get the trunks that held their worldly possessions.

Grandpa decided to build a one-room house on the highest spot of the 40 acres. He tied a rope around tree trunks in both rear corners and ran it under the house eaves to keep the wind from lifting the house. It had only dirt for a floor.

They lived in this house for five years. In the meantime, Grandpa was working on another building that was to be a barn. However, when it was finished they moved into it, as a baby was coming to enlarge their family. My mother was born there October 10, 1885.

They later dug a cellar by hand and built a two-story house over it. The large rocks in the cellar walls provided the foundation for the house. The house had two rooms down and two upstairs, with an open porch across the front. It took some time to get it built because no carpenter was hired. It was a change from the two homes they had lived in previously because it had a floor, which made it much warmer.

Grandfather went about digging a tile ditch by hand. He went to Ser City to get tile. They were also tiling in the city. Workers had dug a ditch across where Grandpa had to drive, and when crossing with the horses and wagon, his wheels fell in the ditch dug for the tile. Grandpa fell from the wagon, which landed on him, breaking his hip. The men tied him to a board and took him home. He was on that board for a long time. He did walk again, but was very crippled.

The ground was worked with a team of horses and walking plow. Sometimes the corn was hoed by hand, not with a cultivator. For meat they would hunt rabbits and prairie chickens, which were frozen and hung on the clothesline during the winter. In summer, Grandpa was busy improving his farmland and buildings.

Forty acres were added to the farm, which is still owned by a member of the family. The original 40 acres has been in the family for more than 100 years. A fifth-generation family member plants and harvests the crops. Grandpa would be so proud if he knew his favorite grandson now owns it.

Mrs. Robert Armstrong
Early, Iowa

Sisters Switched Places

My mother came to the United States from Litenuritz, Czechoslovakia, in 1911.

Her sister had a housekeeping job waiting in Philadelphia, Pennsylvania, but was suddenly taken sick the day before she was to sail. She knew she couldn't go and my grandmother didn't want to lose all the $200 fare, so my mother took her place, using her sister's name and passport. The crossing took 21 days.

While working for some Germans in Philadelphia who took a German paper, my mother read an ad from a widower, Louis Reistle, of Swedesboro, New Jersey, who wanted a housekeeper. My mother answered the ad, and in 1912 married my father Louis.

Gertrude Reistle Myers
Swedesboro, New Jersey

Keeping the Farm in the Family

My father-in-law, George Holzwarth Jr., was born in Rohrbach, Russia, November 8, 1885. His parents were George and Philpine Holzwarth. There were nine children in the family. His parents decided to leave for America because their son, John, would have had to go into the army; the 100 years of no army service promised to German settlers was coming to an end. They sold all of their possessions, took their clothes and money and traveled to Hamburg, Germany. They booked passage on the ship *Columbia* and sailed for America October 25, 1900. They landed in New York on November 5. The thing he remembered most about the ocean trip was everyone's seasickness, though he never got sick himself.

They got on a train and came to St. Francis, Kansas, where they had some relatives who had come here earlier. They had to endure many hardships. George's first job at the age of 15 was herding sheep on a ranch near Haigler, Nebraska. He had to walk 17 miles one way to work. His next job was on the railroad at Haigler, still the same 17 miles to walk.

The inability to speak English was an obstacle. He explained that when they bought something they motioned to what they wanted, then held out their money and let the storekeeper take what they owed.

At the age of 22, George had saved enough to buy homestead rights from a man who had decided to sell for $50. With the help of his brother John, George built a two-room sod house on the 160 acres. This same man told him he knew of a good German girl in South Dakota who needed a husband. George went to Dakota on the train. He met, married and brought Julia Orth home in fewer than three weeks. Thus began a marriage that lasted 56 years, until her death. My mother-in-law told me many years later that she got so homesick she would have walked home, but it was too far.

George and Julia worked hard, and little by little they added buildings and acres to the original homestead, while adding 11 children to the family. There is not room here to tell of the good and bad years: suffice to say they were able to retire to town where they enjoyed many good years. Julia died at 79, George died at 94. I married their son Alvin in 1946. We have lived on this farm for 47 years, and we will pass the farm on to our son, who will hopefully pass it on to his, too.

Marie Holzwarth

St. Francis, Kansas

Fortuneteller's Prediction Came True

The first Jech (yeck) ancestor I am aware of is Václav (vahts-laff) Jech. He was born on January 21, 1832, in either Bohemia or Moravia, which was part of the Hapsburg Empire.

Although Emperor Joseph II abolished serfdom and proclaimed religious freedom in 1781, many of the reforms were ignored by local authorities. The people began a national revival demanding the use of the Czech, rather than German language, the removal of government control of the churches, and the ability to govern themselves. People who advocated change were hunted down mercilessly. The movement culminated in the revolt of 1848. The Hapsburgs were able to quell the rebellion, but not without granting many concessions, including the reduction of taxes, abolition of censorship and general political amnesty. The reforms were short lived, and the cycle of riot, reform and repression continued into the 20th century.

When Václav was a little boy, his father was outspoken against the Catholic Church's involvement in the Austrian government. His father was arrested for his activities and imprisoned for many years. Maybe because of this hardship, Václav never received any formal education. When he was released from prison, his father was in poor health; he died a short time later. The experience angered Václav to the point that he left the Catholic faith. When he had children, they were christened in the Lutheran church. Later, he also changed his name and that of his son, Václav, to Wesley.

Rosalie Vasa was born on November 20, 1844, and lived in Podébrady (puh-dye-brah-dee), a Bohemian village 30 miles east of Prague. The town lies on the river Labe (Elbe) and is noted for its spas, which are particularly effective in treating heart diseases. On the edge of town is a large castle, which was rebuilt during the 16th century Renaissance and again during the baroque period of the 18th century.

Rosalie lived in Podébrady with her parents and at least one sister, Mary. The family had a beautiful home. It was a two-story white stucco with a red tile roof. There were eight to 10 rooms in the house. Connected to one side of the house, also of stucco and tile, was a one-story structure for the livestock. The place was surrounded by a tall picket fence. Directly in front of the house was a carriage gate flanked by tall square stucco pillars. To the left was a small personnel gate. Two small windows on the second story overlooked the gates. Rosalie received a minimal education, attending school for two or three years.

Some time around 1862, a marriage was arranged between Václav, who was nearly 30 years old, and Rosalie, who was about 18. At about the same time, Rosalie's sister, Mary, married a young man by the name of Josef Maly. Both young couples moved into the Vasa family home. Václav helped them farm.

Over the years, 12 children were born to Václav and Rosalie, but it appears that only six survived to adulthood: Mary, 1863; Joseph, 1864; Rosalie, 1869; Václav, 1873; Premsyl Fred, 1876; and Anna Ella, 1880.

Everyone in the combined families did their share to earn a living. When the adults and older children went to the fields, the younger children were left at home to watch the toddlers. They were told to look out the second floor windows if anyone came to the gate. They were not to unlock the gates for any strangers, especially gypsies. Young Václav recalled that once gypsies did come to the gate.

In 1883, the Jech family left for America. Religious freedom, the threat of war and the promise of more land and space in the new country were probably all contributing factors in their decision. Václav, age 51, and Rosalie, age 39, left for New York with their six children. They left the Malys—who followed in the mid-'90s—behind.

The Jech family arrived in America at the port of New York. While there, a fortuneteller approached Rosalie and offered to look into the future for them. Rosalie consented. The fortuneteller saw a wooden casket tied with a rope. She saw nothing else and couldn't explain what she saw. The Jechs were puzzled, but discounted the vision and left for Kansas.

Arriving in Caldwell, Kansas, they stayed with the Sugelas and Lubedellas for a week or so. They bought a place nine miles west of town.

The oldest daughter, Mary, had married Frank Kubic and was expecting a child in the summer of 1886. There were complications, and she died in childbirth at the age of 23. She was placed in a coffin in the parlor and the family sat watch and grieved. The weather was hot that time of year and the body was not embalmed. The body swelled and began to push the wooden casket apart. They tied the coffin with clothesline to secure it enough to transport it for burial. Thus the fortuneteller's gruesome prediction came to pass.

In 1888 or '89 the Jechs sold the Kansas place and bought a claim near Okarche, Oklahoma Territory, in Kingfisher County. They paid $400 for it and moved there with the five remaining children.

The Malys arrived in Oklahoma about 1897. By now they had six children: five boys and a girl, Mary Maria, who was about 12 years old. They settled in Breckenridge, 20 miles east of Enid near Fairmont in Garfield County. They were 60 to 70 miles from the Jechs.

Over the years the older children married and moved out. Joseph married Mary Sixta. Rosalie married Frank Wewerka. Wesly (young Václav) married Antoinette Springler. On January 23, 1898, Václav passed away.

By 1900, there was just Rosalie, Premsyl Fred and Anna Ella at home. On July 17, Anna married Frank Benjamin Skarky. Premsyl continued to run the farm and care for his mother, which was expected of the youngest son. On November 26, 1903, Premsyl married Mary Maria Maly, and once again the Jechs and Malys shared a home. Mary was 18 and Premsyl, 27.

Sometime between 1900 and 1920, this branch of the Jechs began to spell their name Yeck to ensure the correct pronunciation. Some of the others continued the original spelling and eventually changed the pronunciation to "jeck."

Rosalie passed away on October 25, 1919, and was buried in Okarche. The following year, Premsyl sold the Okarche place and bought a farm near Banner, Oklahoma. He put $25,000 down on the $40,000 selling price. The canceled check was placed in the frame of their hand-tinted wedding picture and remained there throughout their lives. The picture and check passed on to Marie Jech Lingo.

Inez Bramwell
Gentry, Arkansas

A New Life on the Open Range

My Grandpa and Grandma Hager both came from Austria in 1880 to live in this great country of ours. Grandpa had made the trip to America two times previously over a period of seven years, at which time he worked and earned money. While in this country he worked in New York State as a farm laborer, earning and saving money for the last big trip in which he brought his new bride, Grandma, to live with him in America.

No doubt this was a great adventure for both of them. Although they left the beautiful countryside, where they both lived on the shore of Lake Constance, they must have looked with great anticipation toward a new life in America. For five years Grandpa worked on a farm near Troy, New York, saving money for another big move to the Midwest, where they bought land and farmed near Waukee, Iowa. During this time they became the parents of four children, two girls and two boys. They lived there for 18 years and later bought land near Perry, Iowa.

The move from Waukee to the farm near Perry in 1903 must have been exciting for the family, as it was near 50 miles in all. No graveled roads, no automobiles, no trucks; just 50 miles over trails that could almost be called open range. The move took five days in all, moving farm implements, livestock and household goods by horse-drawn wagons. My father, who was 13 years old at the time, rode herd on the cattle.

After 18 years on that farm, Grandpa and Grandma retired and moved to Perry. They both missed their beautiful native country, but never had the opportunity to return for a visit before their deaths in 1931.

Francis E. Hager
Sun City, Arizona

Both Citizenship and Ancestry Treasured

As I grow older, I have many regrets. One is that I never listened more when Mother talked about coming to America from the old country.

She was born in a small farming village of Bohemia near Prague, or Praha. The village of Chrudim (we thought of it as Rodheim) was about 20 miles from the capital of Bohemia-Praha.

Their house was small, half of it being a barn for the poultry and animals. Grandfather would walk out each day to the sugar beet fields to work, often 16 to 18 hours a day. Another principal crop of that area was hops, from which the famous Pilsner beer was made.

Mother often spoke of tending the geese. Goose or carp is the traditional Christmas dinner entrée. The feathers were also an important factor in the family's comfort. The feathers were plucked and "stripped" for pillow down and "featherbeds," which were similar to our present-day comforters.

Mother and her brother, Rudolph, were the only two of 17 children to reach adulthood. Most died in infancy, with the exception of one, little Tony, who lived to be 5.

The soil was rich, and farming was one of the main occupations. Grandfather was a farmer and a shoemaker for the castle at Prague. He was also a musician; I remember him trying to teach us to play the violin.

Much of the land was forest, which was always neat and clean because the frugal peasants gathered up any broken branches for fuel. Most of the land belonged to either the nobility or the German rulers; the peasants were reduced to serfdom.

This period of time preceded the great European depression of 1907. It was then that my grandfather decided to leave for America, where he could work for himself and be free from constant fear and pressure. Stories circulated about America, where the streets were paved with gold, and roasted pigs, complete with knives and forks, ran down the streets!

A Mr. Martinek, who left earlier for America, wrote to Grandfather, urging him to come to Cedar Rapids, Iowa. At that time Mr. Martinek owned a tin shop on 16th Avenue West, now commonly referred to as Little Bohemia, 16th Avenue. I never heard how he reached Cedar Rapids.

Grandfather worked at the T.M. Sinclair Packing Plant—later Wilson's—in Cedar Rapids and saved enough money to bring his family over. It was common practice then for one to come to America, save his money, and bring another over, then another.

Grandfather didn't send money, but tickets. As soon as the tickets arrived, Grandmother gathered up what they could carry in bags and bundles. With my 12-year-old mother and 2-year-old Rudolph, the trio walked the 20 miles to the train station that night.

There they took the fourth-class "immigrant" train, which took them to the harbor city of Hamburg, Germany. A shuttle train of some sort took them to their ship. I recall Mother speaking of the North Star, which could have been either the name of the line or the ship itself.

They went by steerage, which Webster defines as, "a section in a passenger ship for passengers paying the lowest fares, and given inferior accommodations—located near the rudder."

Between 1892 and 1932, 85 to 95 percent of all immigrants to the United States came by steerage. It was the responsibility of the steamship company to prepare the immigrants' manifests, made up of the famous 29 questions. These were set up by the United States, composed primarily of name, nationality, trade, destination, health, name of sponsor, and how much money they had—usually $30.

The cost of the trip was around $30 at that time, which paid for everything, including food. They were hustled, bag and baggage, to a lower deck, then to one below that, the orlop deck. Imagine a large room about seven feet high, as wide as the ship and one-third its length, located in the bow or stern. Floors and ceilings were iron or wood. Through the center there was a shaft to the hold. A framework of iron pipes formed tiers of two-by-six berths. The beds were made up of metal strips with straw-stuffed burlap for mattresses. The rooms—which held about 300—were duplicated on other parts of the ship. This section of the ship experiences the most violent motion, dirt from the stack and odors from the hold and galleys.

The immigrants ate from shelves or benches in passages of the sleeping compartments. The toilets and washrooms were inadequate; only saltwater was available. The inadequate ventilation, foul air, vomit of the seasick, odor of unwashed bodies and the stench of the nearby toilets made one nauseous.

Many just lay in a stupor caused by the foul air—there was no fresh air—and the continual babble of tongues. There was a very small deck where they could sometimes go outside.

The fatality rate for steerage ran about 10 percent. Mother told of bodies—mostly those of old people or young children—being slipped into the sea at night.

Each passenger was issued a plate, cup and spoon. The food was thin soup and stringy beef. Many didn't eat, or just couldn't. Utensils, hands and faces were washed in cold saltwater in the same basin or barrel.

One group was avoided because of their thieving habits. They would sit on the deck, combing lice from their long, dark hair. In such close quarters, everyone had lice. When the ship docked, these people appeared in beautiful black dresses and gold jewelry.

This trip across the ocean took two to three weeks. Imagine living under these conditions for that period of time! How happy everyone was as they crowded on deck to see the Statue of Liberty! They were awed by the "Great Lady."

As they left the ship at Ellis Island with their bags and bundles, they wore a tag around their necks proclaiming their name and manifest number. They were ushered into a large registry hall— more than 200 feet long and 100 feet wide, with a 56-foot vaulted ceiling. In this hall was a maze of passageways with iron-pipe railings called "the pens," separating the immigrants by ship or manifest number. The immigrants waited there for their manifests to be checked. Interpreters speaking 15 different languages helped them through their examinations.

During the three-day routine quarantine, baggage was disinfected, and everyone was examined for possible contagious diseases such as scarlet fever, measles, diphtheria, and more particularly for the five epidemic diseases: cholera, plague, smallpox, typhus and yellow fever.

Here they also were checked for ailments such as chronic alcoholism, trachoma and any form of tuberculosis or mental deficiency. Anyone with one of these, or any physical disability that would prevent them from earning a living, would be deported.

Then the immigrants had to wait for friends, money or directions telling them where to go. Fortunately, my grandmother had a pre-paid train ticket. An interpreter saw that she, her children and their baggage got on the right train—to Cedar Rapids.

Grandfather met them there and took them to the house of some Bohemian friends to stay for the time being. Later, they bought a large two-story house on 15th Avenue, which had been moved in from lower Third at about 10th Avenue.

Mother went to school for about a year. When she turned 13, her parents decided that it was time she earned some money, so she went to work in the Quaker Oats Company packaging department.

Her forelady, "Josie," liked her, and told her that if she went back to school for a while to learn more of the language, she could become a forelady too.

Her folks thought the idea was "foolish." She had to earn money, so she didn't return to school. She stopped at the dime store each payday to buy a pretty cut-glass goblet—she liked pretty things. I have the one remaining goblet. The rest of the money—her wages—her father took, as did many fathers of that day.

My mother and father met at the Quaker Oats plant where both worked. Despite the language barrier, love conquered all; they were married when she was only 17.

Mother's brother, Rudolph, went on to school, but like most boys and girls in that day, he went only until he was 16. Then, like all good Czech people, he went to work at the packing house. Men's factory wages here were about $4 per week. Like Mother, most of his wages went to their father.

He received his first citizenship papers; one had to get one's final papers within seven years. I remember Mother reminding him he had to pay his "head tax," which was $1 every year.

Originally, the tax was 50 cents. By 1891, it was $1. By 1918, the tax was $8. This money was used for the administration of the immigration service. Mother became a citizen when she married my father, and thus was exempt from the tax. The tax was abolished in 1952, when it was replaced by a $25 visa.

One day Uncle Rudolph received a letter from the Czech government, informing him that he had to return to Czechoslovakia for military service because he was still an official citizen of his homeland. It was nearly time for his first papers to expire.

I was 14 at the time. How I worked with him so he could pass his citizenship test! To pass, one must know more about our government than most ordinary citizens do—the making of laws, senate, congress, etc. When he received his papers, he gave me a Bulova wristwatch that I treasured for years; I still have the battered remains.

My father was Irish. His family had been here for generations, but he always told us children that Mother was special. She came from "across the water." I suspect that is the reason why our family cherishes our Czech ancestry.

Helen Stevens
Cedar Rapids, Iowa

Couple Endured Rough Journey to America

My grandpa was born in Poland Russia in 1852. He met his spouse in a village where he went for a haircut. She was taking care of children there for $9 a year. At 19, Grandpa married Grandma, 16, and they left for America.

They left Antwerp, Belgium, November 24, 1874. There were 628 Mennonites aboard their ship, the SS Vaterland. This group had an unusually rough journey. The ship was badly damaged due to violent storms. It lost three propeller blades. The first in the English Channel, the second halfway across. They kept limping along till they neared the United States, where the last one was lost. The ship's voyage took 21 days.

When they started out the weather was nice. Everything went fine until midnight, when they collided with another ship. The ship wasn't damaged seriously but needed repairs. They returned to London. After six days the ship was ready to go, but smallpox broke out among the children in eight families. They were ordered to leave harbor at once. The sick children were transferred to a hospital ship, where two lost their lives in the transfer. They sailed out five miles from the harbor and remained there till they were released.

En route the seas became so boisterous and the waves so violent that they clapped together above the ship. The machinery was damaged to the extent they could not continue. Word was sent to London, Liverpool and Antwerp. The damaged ship turned around and started limping back to Liverpool. An American liner came to their rescue. While transferring passengers from the damaged ship to the American, water rushed in to where they thought the ship would sink. The lifeboats were filled. Thirty-five passengers did not find room in the lifeboats and had to remain on the sinking ship. They cried to God to have mercy on them and receive their souls. During their greatest distress a sailor went down into the ship to see how far they were from filling with water. The sailor came back up and said the ship would not sink. There was another wall that prevented the water from filling the entire bottom of the ship. Their ship was towed back to Queenstown.

Grandma and Grandpa arrived at Hutchinson, Kansas, at 11:00 on a cold wintry night when the temperature was 12 below zero. They wandered about the streets of a strange country—penniless, hungry and homeless—until a man came along and opened an empty store building for their whole party to crowd into.

Grandpa and Grandpa eventually settled in McPherson county in Lontree township, so-called for its lone tree. They had $5 to start out with. There was grass five feet high, and there were no trees or buildings. Grandpa hired a man with a team of oxen to plow the sod. He also built a sod house. The lumber for the windows, doors and roof had to be hauled with oxen from Halstead, as McPherson had no lumberyard, only three shacks. Grandpa had to quit working on the roof before it was finished in order to earn some money and make a living. While he was gone, there was thunder and lightning and rain. Mother, with the children, would move from one side of the house to the other to keep from getting wet. A tin can with tallow and a wick in it was the only way of lighting the house.

One time Grandpa had a team of barn horses he tried to break in. When he couldn't handle them alone, he called for Grandma's help. With her holding onto the lines, they stumbled along in a field of hand-cut corn. The horses ran onto the corn pile, pulling Grandma along. They threw her against a pointed cornstalk, which cut about a four-inch gash in her side. Grandpa brought her a mirror to look at her wound. When she saw her own intestines, she fainted.

An old man took seashells the size of a hand and scraped the insides, which produced a powder that he applied to the wound. It healed, despite her being big with child. She didn't miscarry, either. This showed how God cared for them.

Another time one of their children was very ill. Sure the child would die, Grandpa found some boards, nailed them together and placed them outdoors. When the little life fled, the corpse would be placed on the table and packed in ice, as the custom was then. However, God saw fit to heal that illness.

There were no innerspring mattresses, only hay in the corner of the room to sleep on. Grandma wore two slips under her dress in the daytime, one of which she would shed at night to spread on the straw for a little protection. Later, boards were nailed together to hold the straw between them, forming a modern bed. Unfortunately, this didn't keep the rats away, and they annoyed the children.

When it got too hot in the straw at night, Grandpa often would go into the yard and find a place where the breeze would blow. With two bricks for a pillow, he would sleep. Sometimes some of the children followed him outside and slept on the ground too. In the morning, Grandma would look pitifully at their eyes, swollen shut due to insect bites. Sometimes their mouths were swollen shut too, so they couldn't eat all day. There were no doctors or money, so they had to trust their care to the Lord.

Sometimes Grandpa wouldn't get the pay due him. He walked to Lindsborg to work, staying all week. One time he walked home with only a few ears of corn. Another time he received a runty little pig. Both times he walked home weeping because he knew he had a hungry family waiting at home. It was on one of these weekends that he found Grandma with a new baby, three days old. She and Grandpa were so hungry, and there was nothing to eat. She got out of bed and soaked some cornmeal with water, putting it on the stove to dry a little. Grandpa was so hungry that he could scarcely wait to stave off the awful hunger.

When the Alto mill at Halstead was built, Grandpa worked there. He also raised pigeons. He had as many as 200 pairs, and he knew them all. The squabs were taken to town to sell. It was a good business. When the pigeons were real hungry at their night-time feeding, Grandpa would say it was a sign of bad weather.

Grandpa fathered 16 children and lived to be 91 years old. Grandma died at 82; she was more feeble. She never learned to read, so Grandpa would read to her. She loved to mend, and she lovingly mended things for her grandchildren in her late years. She never went to a doctor or a dentist, and never wore glasses.

Mrs. Gilmore Unruh
Moundridge, Kansas

Wool Grew on Stalks in America

Daddy was born on a boat coming to America in 1880. His parents came from the Polish part of Germany, which had yet to become Poland. They were farmers, and they heard that "you could grow wool on stalks and get rich" in America. When they said "wool," they were referring to cotton.

Anton Ribitzki, my dad, said his name meant "Little Fish." Our family wanted to check out the papers on their immigration to New York but found the records covering the years we needed had been burned. We know they migrated to Lawrence, Tennessee, where daddy was the "big man of the town." We have to laugh, though, because the "big man" was just 5 years old! Maybe "popular little boy" would have suited him better. From Tennessee the Ribitzki's went to Bremond, Texas. Grandpa got a farm in Rosebud, Texas, and walked there. We were told he won the farm gambling, but we can't be sure. Anyway, he got the farm and raised my daddy there.

When Daddy went to school he spoke Polish but the school and the priest were German, so Daddy learned to pray in German, rather than Polish.

It was customary to go to house dances, so Daddy went to one. There he danced with Veronica Canik, a Czech girl who was just 14; Daddy was 36. They said if she danced with him it meant she'd marry him. So she did.

Daddy and Mama had 15 children; I am one of the middle children. We grew up working on the farm, and when we wanted to rest in the field we'd try to get Daddy to tell us stories, but it didn't work very well, 'cause he'd just tell us quickly and get us back to work.

All of us were born at home and grew up speaking Czech, Mama's language. Daddy spoke Polish, Czech, German and also learned English. Mama didn't speak English very well at first, but she learned to speak it better later.

Trudy Cook
Huffman, Texas

Brothers' Run on Oklahoma Land Successful

Elizabeth Kele was born in the town of Meskolisi, state of Borsod Megye, Hungary, on July 14, 1879. Little did her parents, Jonas and Barbolia Roscsie Kele, know of the adventure that lay in store for this tiny child. She had two sisters, Barbara and Mary.

Elizabeth's husband came to America first. They had two children, Joseph and little Elizabeth. She never heard from him again.

Later, family friends Charley, Frank, and Michael Kiss—who were brothers—Michael's wife Theresa and Elizabeth's sister Mary booked passage on a ship to the New World. Families said goodbye again, this time with heavy hearts.

This story had a happier ending. The five immigrants arrived in New York some time before 1893. Their hearts were filled with wild hopes and dreams of things they could accomplish in their new land. They spoke no English. The early years were frightening and difficult.

Mary found work in New York and stayed there. The others worked their way west. In 1893, they heard of the Cherokee Strip Land Run in Oklahoma and made their way there to participate. The men made the run safely, but Theresa died in childbirth during it. Each brother received 160 acres of land, located southwest of what is now Alva, Oklahoma.

They worked the land, saving what they could and establishing their homesteads. Mike remarried. His second wife drank bad water without boiling it and died of typhoid.

Mary sent Elizabeth money, asking her to come to America and bring Mary's children. Elizabeth agreed. Mary signed for her, and in 1908 Elizabeth arrived in New York on a ship with Mary's children.

Mary kept in touch with Mike in Oklahoma. She wrote to him, telling him that Elizabeth had brought her children over, but that Elizabeth's children were still in Hungary.

Sometime later, Mary and Elizabeth received proposals of marriage from Mike and Frank, saying they would pay expenses to bring the children over, plus the train fare west, if the women would accept their proposals and join them. Elizabeth signed for and made arrangements for Barbara's husband, Mr. Pancek, to bring Joseph and Elizabeth over. He left his family behind.

Charlie and Frank had changed the spelling of their name to Kish, the American pronunciation of Kiss. Elizabeth and Frank were married in 1909. To this union four children were born: Rose, Emma, Mary and Frank. Rose was my husband's mother.

Four years later Frank Sr. was killed while breaking a wild horse. It threw him and trampled him. He left Elizabeth pregnant, with five other children to raise alone.

She cleaned houses, did washings and ironings and any work she could to care for her family. She homesteaded a piece of land in New Mexico, then sold it when she could. She worked in the sugar beet fields in Saginaw, Michigan. The children went to work at young ages. They moved to Ohio and returned to Oklahoma in 1918.

Elizabeth died in 1984 at the age of 85. She still walked four blocks to daily mass two years before she died. Mary died in 1937, Mike in 1947 and Charley died in California. Mr. Pancek was never able to get his family here. He lost his mind from grief and loneliness. Barbara remained in Hungary.

La Donna Berry Ring
Alva, Oklahoma

Always Happy in the New World

Reprinted courtesy of the Thousand Oaks *News Chronicle*.

Ursula Riccio was a 14-year-old girl from Austria who had only a trunk of clothes and "one coin" when she went through Ellis Island, alone, on her way to Connecticut.

"It was a big building full of people," she recalled in an Austrian accent. "All the people were lined up against the walls and were sitting with their feet up."

Riccio's father came to the United States around the turn of the century and wanted to bring his wife, son and four daughters to his new country.

He returned to Austria with hopes of selling the family farm in Thorlmagoern, but he couldn't find a buyer.

Times were tough, Riccio, 96, recalled. Her father found work in a lumber mill. While working to earn money to get his family to the United States, part of his hand was cut off in an accident at the mill.

U.S. officials classified Riccio's father as handicapped because of his injury and he was barred from immigrating.

Instead, he sent his wife and children to the United States.

Riccio traveled across Germany alone. Her mother, brother and sisters had earlier gone to the United States.

The Austrian teenager had no shoes. Her father gave her some money and told her to buy shoes along the way.

Not knowing a great deal about shoes, Riccio bought some comfortable bedroom slippers in Germany and wore those during her cross-Atlantic trip.

Her introduction to United States in 1908 was a quick lesson in the hard, cold realities of her new country.

Riccio had a favorite red ring. She took it off and placed it on a shelf while washing her hands at Ellis Island. When she finished washing her hands, the ring was gone.

Even finding her family at a train station was not without risk. Riccio was to meet her family in Connecticut. It was October, and she had not seen her family since they had left the previous January.

She looked through the train station.

She looked and looked.

So did her sisters.

Finally, a young girl walked up and gave her a vague look of recognition.

She asked, "Are you Ursula?"

"I didn't recognize my own sister," Riccio said.

Dress styles were much different in Connecticut than they were in Austria, she said. Her family had changed much in the New World.

Riccio didn't bring far-flung dreams or romantic images of life in the United States when she left Austria.

When asked what was on her mind as she traveled to the United States, she replied: "I hope it's a nice country. As long as my family is there, I'll make it nice."

She added, "I've always been happy since I've been here."

Riccio has lived in Thousand Oaks since 1961. She has a daughter and a son, seven grandchildren and 17 great-grandchildren.

Submitted by Mary Nelson
Thousand Oaks, California

The Chain Remains Unbroken

I hope you will consider my story about my father, Vincent Gondol Jr. This is a reverse story. He was born on February 23, 1911, at Youngstown, Ohio. His Hungarian parents, Vincent Gondol Sr. and Esther, had settled upon coming to the United States. When my father was 18 months old, my grandmother took him and his sister to Tiszatarjanban, Miskolc, Hungary. My father lived in Hungary for 15 years, while the communist were rounding up all the young men for the military. My grandmother told him, "You are an American citizen, go to the United States." Although my grandmother lived in a communist country, she did not want her son fighting in its army; she just didn't believe in communist ways.

In 1928, my grandmother saved money to pay her son's ship fare. My father left Hungary at 4:30 in the morning; the entire town's population showed up to see him leave for the United States, the land of freedom. Even the band played while he was leaving. My father came back to the United States and didn't know one word of English.

On the ship, my father was seasick for days. He spent all of his money on the ship, even the money for his train ticket when he reached Ellis Island in New York. He stayed with some nuns until his uncle, Steve Adam, sent him money to buy his train ticket to Lorado, Logan County, West Virginia. He arrived at Lorado on November 29, 1928.

He had a job waiting for him at the mines in Lorado. He learned English while he worked; he didn't attend school here. My father didn't have a diploma or a degree. He mastered English but never lost his Hungarian accent.

He married my mother, Julia Ann Kohari, on August 25, 1934. My sister, Julia Esther, was born on September 20, 1935; I was born on January 29, 1939.

My father retired from the mines in 1964. He and my mother moved to North Palm Beach, Florida. During the 1970s, my father's nephew's son, Béla, came to Michigan on an agricultural program. My father sent him a round-trip plane ticket to Florida, and they got to spend a week or two together. When it came time for Béla to go back to Michigan to join his group returning to Hungary, my father told him, "Stay here in the United States." Béla told him, "I have to go back to Hungary. If I don't, my country will send my parents to Siberia."

On December 8, 1981, my father died. His ashes were spread on the Atlantic Ocean. I would like to think they reached Hungary once again, as he always wanted to go back there for a visit.

In September 1992, Béla died. Today I write to Béla's 14-year-old daughter, Katalin. I am so thankful to have her to correspond with; it means that the chain isn't broken. It's like having a part of my father again!

Elizabeth "Gondol" Walls
Kistler, West Virginia

Good Health and Good Life in America

The year was 1873, the place Dornbirn, Austria. Josef Meusburger, in his early 20s, left his home, family and friends to live the rest of his life in the United States of America.

He left Dornbirn by train on March 29, 1873. There was a ship waiting at Bregenz with many emigrants. They joined Josef and were then transported by train to Mannheim, by ship to Koln, and again by train to Bremen, where they spent two days waiting for another train to Bremerhafen. The train was packed with people old and young, and there was much jockeying to see who would be first off and loaded in the small boats that would deliver them to the German ship *Deutsland,* which was anchored out in the bay.

They departed Bremerhafen that day for Southhampton, England, where they loaded up on coal. On Tuesday they left for the United States in a heavy thunderstorm. The waves were huge, and many people were seasick; children cried all day and night. Altogether there were about 1,000 people on the ship.

They arrived in New York on April 18, and after exchanging their money for American currency, Josef and the others were transported by train to Troy, New York, to work as farm laborers. Wages were $18 a month. Josef hired out to a farmer for that amount and later was paid $20. No one spoke German, so Josef had to learn English, which turned out to be no problem as he was a fast learner. Josef complained in a letter to his family in Austria that it was cold until the middle of May and then it turned unbearably hot in June. He had to rise at 3:00 every morning to milk the cows; he milked them again at noon. Three meals a day were furnished with plenty of meat, which suited him.

He loved the beauty of his surroundings: the large mountains in the distance and plenty of hills nearby. He never regretted coming to America but reported that some did. He considered the pay good and reported that he was making more money here than he could ever make in his home country. He was proud that he could make good money, and he was able to repay his family the money he had borrowed to make the trip.

After being in America for two years he wrote to his family and reported that there was a slowdown in available work. He was being paid $25 a month, and his earnings for the previous year amounted to $260. The possibility that he may be out of work prompted him to consider moving to Iowa. He also reported that cattle prices were very high—approximately $100—and that hay was cheap. Wages for girls were very low, $2 a week, although in his hometown girls would only be paid 2 cents.

Josef moved to Iowa in 1876 or '77. In a letter to his brother dated Waukee, Iowa, May 16, 1880, he stated that he was in his fifth year working for the same man—wages were $18 a month, the same as in Troy, New York. His job was to take care of eight horses, 20 cows, 20 oxen and about 100 pigs. Most of his time was spent in the fields walking behind two horses.

A letter to his brother in Austria dated Waukee, Iowa, February 28, 1886, revealed that Josef was now married, as he reported living with his in-laws the previous year. He had bought some land and sold 80 acres to his father-in-law for $2,200; he in turn bought 160 acres for $5,000. His acreage had a roomy house, a big barn and 300 trees—a very beautiful place. He said that Joseph Hager, my grandfather, lived and farmed only a short distance from his farm.

He mentioned that he and his family—two girls and one boy—were in good health. His farm operation was as follows: five horses, two cows, two calves, three pigs and 50 chickens. Quoting from his letter, "I have never regretted that I came to America. I have made it good in this country—I have enough land to plant on and my children will never get hungry and starve. The main thing is that we stay healthy. In Germany I never would have accomplished what I have here."

Francis E. Hager
Sun City, Arizona

Mormon Leader Gave Grandpa Advice

My maternal grandfather, Nicholas Klotz, was born in Austria. From the beginning, Grandpa Klotz had an exciting life. In the early 1800s Austria was taken over by Napoleon. Grandpa remembered an octagon-shaped fort with portholes and a stone-slabbed roof. It was used in times when raiders came through the Brenner Pass, near where the family lived. At one time Austria was one of the most powerful countries in Europe, but by the time he was born, the country had been through many wars. Each time Austria suffered greatly and lost some of its territory.

The Austrian people grew tired of war. In 1847, Joseph Ludwig Schneller, an uncle of Grandpa's who was a sea captain, ship owner and importer/exporter, fitted a sailing vessel for a trip to America. About July 11, Captain Schneller set sail with members of the Klotz and Schneller families, including 6-year-old Nicholas.

The Klotz family settled in Fond du Lac county, where Grandpa received whatever education he could in the common schools of the area. His father was a firm believer in education, so when his brother-in-law, Father Anton Schneller, suggested Nicholas come to New York and attend St. John's College at Fordham, he gave his permission. Grandpa always said he received five years of education in the two years that he was at St. John's.

Nicholas returned to Wisconsin to work on his father's farm, but in 1858, when he was 17, he began the adventure of his lifetime. His uncle, Captain Schneller, who had brought the families to America, offered him a trip to California on his sailing vessel.

The only complete water route at that time was around Cape Horn at the southern tip of South America, which was still a primitive country. Naked natives were a common sight along the shores. Theirs was not one of the new clipper ships that made the trip in 100 days or fewer. Their journey took a year, and they had to endure as many as 200 days of boredom and seasickness. Despite the drawbacks, thousands of gold-seekers were willing to pay

$300—a large amount in those days—to reach California. The alternative was a land-sea route through the jungles of the Isthmus of Panama. With the best connections, this route could be negotiated in as few as eight weeks if the traveler survived the hardships and tropical diseases. Also, they often waited many weeks for a ship out of Panama City bound for San Francisco.

When Captain Schneller's ship arrived at San Francisco, ships of every description were riding anchor in the harbor. Of the tens of thousands of prospectors who streamed into California during the gold rush of the late 1840s and 1850s, many arrived in vessels such as these.

Grandpa's experience with horses on the farm helped him secure a job driving freight wagons from San Francisco to Sacramento. Business was booming in Sacramento: the heart of life, trade and vice. Grandpa was a deeply religious man, and apparently he did not succumb to the many vices and temptations. My mother told in later years how, after a day of business in town, he said, "Oh darn, I was going to get a glass of beer when I was in town and I forgot," so surely drinking was not one of his problems.

There were no railroads west of the Mississippi, so freight was hauled in wagon trains. Lone wagons were easy prey to bandits and Indians, which still abounded in that wild country. Grandpa Klotz joined other drivers to form wagon trains—sometimes as many as 25 long—with high-wheeled wagons, each pulled by a team of six to 20 oxen, mules or horses. One man drove his team and also guarded the freight on his wagon. The drivers were called bullwhackers or mule skinners. The wagons lumbered along at a mile or two an hour, making about 100 miles in a seven-day week. There were no Sundays west of Omaha.

When the Civil War began, Grandpa was ready to join the army, as all young men were being conscripted. President Lincoln decided the freight drivers were needed where they were, and he told them to stay on their jobs.

According to family legend, Grandpa told this story of his first trip to Salt Lake City. He had to wait for other wagons to make up a train for the return trip. There was a shortage of help due to the war, and at times a driver had to wait weeks. Having heard of the beautiful Mormon Temple, Grandpa decided to see it while he was waiting. He was amazed to find the entrance guarded by a man "with an Irish brogue so thick you could cut it with a knife."

"How come an Irishman like you came to be a Mormon?" Grandpa asked.

"I'm not a Mormon. I'm a Roman Catholic," the man answered, "but I work here. The Mormons are good people. They mind their business and want you to mind yours. But have you met their leader, Brigham Young?"

The Irishman took Grandpa in to meet the "President" as he was called.

Grandpa spent one winter working on a ranch owned by the Mormons, 160 miles from Salt Lake City. The people he lived with that winter were kind and considerate. Knowing he was Catholic, they never served meat on Friday, nor ate any themselves. This was one of the rules of the church at that time. They surely endeared themselves and the Mormon people to my grandfather.

The rancher had no money, so Grandpa was paid in gold dust, which was carried in a little canvas pouch called a poke. He did very little mining himself. When he got back to Salt Lake City, his pack was stolen. Although he needed and valued the gold, what he considered his greatest treasure was a crucifix that had been a gift from his uncle, Father Schneller. Grandpa told his Irish friend how awful he felt.

"Have you reported it?" the Irishman asked. "There isn't a man comes here that we don't know where he comes from or where he is going. Report it and come back in a few days."

When Grandpa returned, there was his pack. Brigham Young asked to see the precious crucifix, which he examined and handed back with the advice, "Take good care of it. Never lose it again."

By this time the freight line on the railroad was extended to Omaha, and Grandpa was moving closer to home. He had grown to manhood in the West. He loved the country, but his family was in Wisconsin. In 1865 he returned to the farm in the town of Eden. He married, raised a family and was elected a state assemblyman and sheriff of Fond du Lac County.

Paula Delfeld
Brownsville, Wisconsin

A Grandma with True Grit

Ida Aman was born in Austria on November 23, 1868, to Jacobi and Caroline Aman. Jacobi died two years later, and Caroline was left to provide for Weindelin and Ida, his younger sister. Caroline married again to a local farmer friend and had two more children.

As a child Ida had a beautiful singing voice. She acquired a guitar and learned to play and yodel in the Swiss style. Her lilting voice echoed through the mountains and valleys of the Tyrolean Alps where she lived. She became quite popular in the nearby villages.

Caroline died when Ida was in her teens. She kept house and did all of the many tasks that her mother had previously done. She also corresponded with a friend, Josef, who had immigrated to the United States and taken up residence in a Chicago boarding house. She looked forward to going to America and marrying Josef and having a family in Chicago.

When Ida reached 18 she was shocked, bewildered, then infuriated because her stepfather announced his intentions to marry her. He was lonely, needed a wife and companion, and Ida was his most likely choice.

This horrible idea forced Ida to make several quick decisions. She decided she must leave Austria. She sought and received help from her brother Weindelin, who now operated a lace factory in

Feldkirch near the Swiss border. Ida sold what little jewelry and material wealth she could find, and with her suitcase and beloved guitar, fled to the French coast and a new life in America.

Traveling alone, with little or no money, she arrived in Chicago only to find that Josef had left town to find work in St. Louis. She worked at the Chicago boarding house, saving her money to travel to St. Louis. By then she had communicated with Josef, who had found her a job in a boarding house near the railroad roundhouse.

She again performed well as a domestic in her new job and was well liked by all. Josef visited regularly, and she entertained the boarders with singing and playing the guitar. The landlady enjoyed the entertainment but soon became jealous of Ida's popularity. This jealously soon manifested itself when Josef called and was told that Ida was out with another man. This was a bold-faced lie, but Josef didn't know the truth. He was hurt and angry and left, never to return. Ida found out the truth much later.

Knowing little English and alone again in a foreign country, Ida courageously continued to become more social and outgoing. During this time Ida met August Haukap at a local dance hall. This meeting led to others and eventually her only marriage.

August was a happy, loving man and father. Five children were born to the couple: Elizabeth the eldest, August, Wenceslas, Marie and the youngest, William. They were a happy family, yet very poor. August was a hard-working teamster but had a drinking habit—common in those days. After receiving his weekly pay he would stop at the corner saloon and pay his liquor bill. This left much less money for the family expenses. This alcohol abuse caused the family much pain. One fateful morning, August, who also tended and hitched the horses, left the barn late and did not have time for his morning shot of whiskey. He became dizzy and fell from the high seat of the piano-moving wagon. His head and back struck the cobblestone street, and he was carried home by friends. He died several days later, only 37 years old.

Ida, now with five children, was forced again to demonstrate her vast courage and face another challenge in her young life. She washed and ironed laundry, which the children delivered in their little wagon. She sewed and mended for the neighborhood. She was subject to call anytime of the day or night to serve as a midwife. She kept the family together. As the children graduated from elementary school, they found jobs wherever they could, some locally, others in the harvest fields, each contributing their share to the family coffers. All in all there was much love and happiness in this family.

As the children became older they married and left home. Ida and her son, Wenceslas, were left to live together. When he married, Ida lived with Wence and his wife, Rose. During this time Ida continued gardening both flowers and vegetables. She also sewed, quilted, and helped in the household duties. At age 69 Ida broke her hip and was hospitalized, where she contracted pneumonia and died on July 3, 1938. Ida was a loving, caring person to all she met and in turn was equally loved by all.

Ralph Litzsinger
Mountain Grove, Missouri

Immigrant Loved Old World and Elvis Presley

The Bokrovits family came from Budapest, Hungary, in the 1950s. They were partially sponsored by the Presbyterian church.

They all worked hard in the Midwest and eventually prospered. The grandfather was not comfortable speaking English—his favorite form of expression was his violin. The music was heartwarming—especially to a family so far from its roots.

Ida, the mother, had an Old-World style love of beautiful things. Surprisingly, she also fell in love with Elvis Presley and his music. So, along with gilded mirrors, lace, and crystal, she had Elvis Presley records.

Perhaps Ida also admired the way Elvis loved his mother.

The two teenaged Bokrovits sons remembered learning English. The Presbyterian sponsoring family would touch the door and say "door." Bit by bit the boys learned English, while their mother cleaned the house, cooked, or helped out in the home.

Louis was the older of the two sons and enjoyed track in high school. Life was good, but Louis always remembered being in concentration camps as a youngster, and there were certain foods he would not eat. At least one family member died as a result of the camps.

Louis was my cousin Sheila's dad. We remember many good things about him. In my mind's eye I still see him driving sleek cars—he loved convertibles. He also served this country in the army, which is also my branch of service. He was loved by all the family. He and his birth family lived through enormous changes; perhaps the wear-and-tear shortened their lives. Louis will always be special. He was my uncle.

Kevin Miller

Huffman, Texas

Three Cheers for the Statue of Liberty

I was told this story many times by my Uncle Albert Harazim. He lived in Lankin, North Dakota. He was born in the small village of Smrzov, Bohemia Czechoslovakia, on April 21, 1893, the youngest of six children. His parents owned a tract of land equivalent to about 10 acres. They were very hard workers. His father was also a tailor. As soon as his father had an extra $150 and one of the children turned 17, he sent them to the United States. After all the children were sent to the United States, his father decided they should all emigrate. They sold their land and sent their prized possessions in a trunk to the children who were already here. Uncle Albert always liked to tell about coming over on the biggest

German passenger steamer at the time, *The Wilhelm Kaiser II*. It was about 1,000 feet long, 100 feet wide and three stories high. They were on the second story. They were oh so excited when they saw the Statue of Liberty. Everyone who could got up on the deck and yelled and hollered.

A 21-gun salute welcomed them to New York Harbor on July 3. The salute frightened his mother, who said, "Why did we come here? It is a war." They were checked by the doctor on Ellis Island. His mother had broken out from washing in the saltwater on the ship. The doctor thought she might have some disease so they quarantined her. Uncle Albert and his father couldn't understand the language, and they didn't know what had happened to Albert's mother. They sat and cried. After several hours the doctor released her. From there they took the train to Conway, North Dakota, where they were met by Uncle Albert's brother, whom he had never seen because he left home before Albert was born. Uncle Albert was 12 years old when they came here. I used to love to hear him tell us about their trip over the ocean.

Rose Potulny
Fordville, North Dakota

Loyalty to America Runs Deep

My grandfather decided to immigrate to America from Poland by way of Austria and Hungary. How bravely they made that journey with a set of twins, born in Vienna. Trudging those long miles with small children had to be trying. My daddy and his twin brother were only 3 years old when they arrived in America at Ellis Island.

The family settled in the industrialized steel mill country of western Pennsylvania. At Washington my granddad worked scooping large shovelfuls of coke into the roaring fires of an open hearth. I remember seeing a single line of men clad in heavy aprons and hoods to protect their shoulders and faces as they fed the furnaces. Sweating from the extreme heat, each man carried a shovel of coke to add to the blaze.

Later Granddad worked in the blacksmith shop. His cheeks were often red from the heat. Thankful for the religious freedom in America, my grandparents seldom complained of their lot or their lack. They built a large two-story house on Goat Hill and raised four boys and four girls to be loyal Americans.

From boyhood, I recall the unpaved streets, family holiday festivities, and the sweet, sugary seckel pears of Washington. Living there was a happy time for me.

My father met my mother in Detroit, where he was lured by the promise of $5 a day working for Henry Ford. However, when work failed to remain steady, he returned to Washington, Pennsylvania, with Mom and me. My parents opened a grocery store and lunchroom, serving sandwiches, soup and cakes—for which my mom became well known—to the men working in nearby steel mills, coal mines and cattle-slaughtering plants.

Dad helped immigrant friends "get the papers"—meaning their naturalization papers—so eagerly sought. Dad also began making smoked sausage. My brother, a year younger than me, and I helped by cutting and seasoning about 400 pounds of meat a week. I was about 10 then.

Taken in an oil-drilling deal, Dad lost his money. He could not expand his grocery business and lost everything in the Great Depression of the '30s.

My parents taught us to be honest, work hard, have pride and love God. I am so happy to have been born and raised in America— so thankful my grandparents came, impelled by their desire for religious freedom and opportunity in America.

Lee Paul Stanley
By Sybil Austin Skakle
Chapel Hill, North Carolina

Chef Found Steady Work in America

In December 1905, Mama and Papa—recently-married Gustave and Paula—decided to take up their lives in the "Land of Opportunity," possibly to avoid conscription in the army.

They left Budapest, Hungary, for a German port and boarded a steamship headed for America. There was no sponsor for them in America, so they must have had some money. They did have skills: Mama was a hotel cook and Papa, a pastry chef.

Seas were rough. Mama's motion sickness was compounded by her pregnancy. She became very ill, spending most of the 14-day trip in the ship's hospital. Papa remained with the regular passengers. The food wasn't good there, so when he visited Mama, who couldn't stand the sight of the more delicate victuals that she was offered, he gratefully did her a favor and consumed them. He regularly visited her at mealtimes.

Although Papa was Hungarian and Mama was Slovak, they both spoke German, a language common to that European area. After seeing the Statue of Liberty and being released from quarantine, they sought out a German *turnverein*, a bakers' guild where jobs were posted. Papa earned $4 a week for long hours and Mama, $6. They lived in a poor area in lower Manhattan. Some of the other immigrants they met there became lifelong friends. Six years and two children later, seeking the American dream, they opened their own bakeshop in Brooklyn. Papa soon went bankrupt when he trusted people who bought "on credit" and then refused to pay.

In later years, after becoming naturalized, Papa became Head Pastry Chef for the famous Longchamps Restaurant in New York City. Although he took a drastic pay cut, he worked throughout the Depression.

My folks taught us to love and appreciate our wonderful country.

Cecilia Droll
Golden, Colorado

"Look at the Greenhorn"

How did my father get from Ellis Island to a farm in upstate New York, when most young immigrant Jews became peddlers or worked at sewing machines in the garment industry's sweat-shops? I finally found out when I read that one of the many Jewish immigrant aid societies encouraged young Jewish men to go to farms, where they placed them in jobs to get away from the hard-ships and crowded conditions of the city ghettos. When I checked with my father he said that was indeed how he got to the farm. He loved farming and left it only because my mother hated life on the farm. My mother also escaped the sweatshops. She worked as a waitress at a hotel in the Catskills before they married. Since the clientele was largely Jewish, language was no problem.

Papa was the first of his siblings to arrive in America. There was no one here to greet him. A Jewish immigrant aid society filled that slot. When he left Poland his father said that he was sorry he hadn't given him a more *goyish*, or worldly, education to better equip him for the New World. The standard education for Jewish boys was heavily religious. Mama's brother was already here and married. She came into his home when she arrived and was expected to share in the work of the house and his little grocery store under the Ninth Avenue El (elevated train) in New York City. His wife was the "mean sister-in-law. She wouldn't let me sit down for a minute. Not even long enough to clean my finger-nails," my mother said.

They left the Old Country as teenagers, never to see their parents again. It took months for a letter to get across the ocean in the days before airmail. Mama would open the infrequent letters with trem-bling hands, pining for word of home. She read them over and over until the pages fell apart at the folds.

Papa and Mama were introduced a year or two after they landed on Ellis Island. Not by a *shadkhn*, or matchmaker, whom many immigrants still used to make matches for their sons and daughters, but through friends and relatives. They considered matchmaking part of the social requirements of the immigrant community where young eligibles were strangers, unlike the homeland *shtetl*, or village, where everyone knew everyone else.

When I came along my sister was already 6 years old and my parents had been in the country for 12 years. By that time their English was adequate, albeit accented. They were active citizens in our town of 18,000; Mama went to every PTA meeting, and Papa was a small businessman. They always voted.

Papa drove a big truck 60 miles each way in the wee hours of the morning two or three times a week to pick up coops of fresh, live poultry at the Washington Market in New York City. He could sell these fresh-killed chickens in his meat and poultry store. He was not a kosher butcher, but the *shochet*, or ritual Jewish slaughterer, came to his market to slaughter chickens according to the dietary laws set out in Leviticus for the Jewish women who kept kosher homes.

My cousin, Sylvie, came over when she was 10. Before she left Poland she saw a picture of my older sister with her American Buster Brown haircut. Sylvie wanted to look like an American girl when she arrived. She sneaked away and had her long hair cut off to match my sister's, much to the chagrin of her mother and our grandmother. When she got here the family helped prepare her for school. My mother's contribution was gym bloomers, which were the required clothing for the mandatory gym classes in New York City schools. Sylvie, apparently a woman of taste and one not easily imposed upon even at that age, made a face when she saw this unattractive garment. My mother, taking umbrage at her audacity, said, *"K Kick nor un de greena,"* which literally means "look at the greenie," short for greenhorn, the label given to immigrants. The clear implication was that Sylvia had no right to look a gift horse in the mouth.

Sylvie's brother, Nathan, was 13 when they came. He went to high school in Brooklyn, where he played football. He was too timid to tell the teacher he could not see the blackboard. She called him to her desk and asked why he did so well on exams when they were printed on a page and so poorly when the questions were on the blackboard. He told her he had poor eyesight and could not see the blackboard. She asked if there was anything she could do to help him. He said yes, she could give him a copy of the questions when she put them on the blackboard. That was a turning point for him, and at age 85, he still remembers Mrs. Jonas. Shortly after, he was declared legally blind, but refused to accept government disability payments because he chose to be independent. He went to work as a copy boy and rose to become president of the company. Later he owned a printing company that printed the *Financial Analyst Journal*.

Papa was succeeded in his business by a younger brother, Joseph, and later two sisters, Fanny and Rose. The families stuck together and helped one another in their new country. The two brothers pledged to each other that whoever "made it" would always help the other. They both helped their sisters' families in times of economic stress. When hardship befell Sylvie's family she came to live with us. My father gave her a job in his store so she could work to send money home to her family, rather than having them feel beholden for family charity.

When my father lost his business in the Great Depression and Aunt Rose's husband lost his job, they went to work for Uncle Joseph in the wholesale chicken yards at West Washington Market. They unloaded chickens coops from the trains that came in from the farms. A side benefit was the unending supply of eggs for our families.

Thirteen of my parent's sisters and brothers stayed behind in Poland. They all perished in the Holocaust except for one cousin, who was hidden all through those years by a Christian woman whom he subsequently married. He asked his dead parents for forgiveness for marrying out of the faith.

Constance Lindemann
Norman, Oklahoma

—■—

Chapter Five: Western European Heritage

Blacksmith Plied Trade in New World

My father, Emil Markobrad, was born in the late 1800s in Virginmost, Yugoslavia, which at that time was part of the Austria-Hungary Empire. At 16 he was aware that he would be enrolled in the army at 18, so, like many other young men his age, he made many efforts to get passage fare to America.

At that time, he was an apprentice blacksmith in Belgrade. His training provided him with a livelihood the rest of his working years. His sister, husband and nephew were living in Pennsylvania, working to make enough money to return to their native county, which they eventually did. They helped Emil accumulate enough money to book passage on a trip here.

Father's only presentable item of clothing was a new hat, of which he was so proud. Alas, when they reached the Statue of Liberty, the rushing onlookers jostled his hat, which flew into the ocean.

After having a difference of opinion with his sister, he left and worked his way west, settling in Youngstown, Ohio. He claimed he learned English there. "That is where I learned to speak so well," he said, although he had a decided brogue all his life. Eventually he landed in Maxwell, New Mexico, where he married our mother, Josephine Mumford, and brought nine children into the world. I am the oldest. Emil moved his family to Wyoming in 1928.

Martha Thompson
Pine Bluffs, Wyoming

Sad Losses at Sea

My grandparents were Frederick Stegman, born November 8, 1840, and Elsie Elizabeth Schenk, born March 17, 1844. They came to America from Switzerland around 1867. They had two little girls and two little boys. A friend whose family was sailing later asked my grandparents to also bring their child, as the vessel they were sailing on was full to capacity.

My grandparents' vessel encountered terrible storms. It sprang a leak, and everyone able had to work at the pumps. Grandmother took her turns. Smallpox broke out on board, and starvation stalked the passengers. Grandmother somehow got food to some of the isolated passengers, many of whom were confined to their rooms.

My grandparents' two little girls died and had to be buried at sea. The child they were bringing for the friend also died. To Grandma it was a terrible thing to have to tell her friend, especially since she would be unable to point out his burial place. She carried the dead little body in her arms, hoping to have him buried when they landed. But when the suspicious captain raised his hood, he stopped the ship, and the boy, too, was buried at sea.

They finally landed at Ellis Island, but you can be sure it was not a happy landing for my dear, heroic grandparents.

Jeanette Wible
Phoenix, Arizona

Wrong Boat Created Communication Problems

My great-grandfather on my mother's side was Ferdinand Koeliker, who married Jeger Kungunde. He was born March 3, 1836.

Great-Grandpa Koeliker was the county male goat keeper in their area of Switzerland. He kept the only male goat for the county. The females were brought to him for breeding. This was his livelihood.

My Great-Aunt Seraphine worked in a silk mill. Her husband

abused her so badly that she took her 2-year-old son and jumped into a river from a cliff. Both drowned. The child was found the next day and Seraphine was found nine days later. Her husband was jailed because of his ill treatment of her. He hid a match in his hair and set the jail on fire. It burned to the ground. He was put in jail in another town and not allowed to go to his wife's funeral. She was known as a beautiful woman.

My Great-Grandfather Ferdinand Koeliker had a daughter, Lina, who was born September 22, 1867. She married Emil Gaugler from Hochwald and Biiren, Switzerland.

My Grandfather Gaugler had a sister, Rose. Their families came to the United States together in 1906. My mother was only 6 months old. When the two couples and all their children went to embark for the United States they went to a boat—but not the right boat! They spoke only German—but got on an Italian boat.

They could not communicate with anyone on the boat except by gestures, which didn't work too well! They had brought some food with them, but the best my mother could tell was that they did not even get into the dining room. By feeding her chopped dried fruits they had and, I presume, some other foods—perhaps my grandmother nursed—my mother survived.

Aunt Rose and her family stayed in New Jersey but my grand-parents—perhaps lured by the promise of work—moved to Erie, Pennsylvania. Eventually Aunt Rose's daughter and son-in-law and two children moved to Erie, too. That daughter is still living in California.

When I was in college in Nyack, New York, I spent the week-end with Great Aunt Rose and Great Uncle Casil when I could. That was more than 50 years ago. During one of my visits, she said to me in her broken English: "I like it here. In this country the woman is the boss." I'm not sure she was 100 percent right on that!

Mrs. Arlene Futrell
Stokes, North Carolina

Couple Found Love at Sea

One of the better aspects of aging is the pleasure of remembering, not only the things you have witnessed, but true-life stories passed along by those who lived them. Take, for instance, the one about Mama and Papa and how they met.

In the 19th century, life in Italy was quite stereotypical. Like most of his contemporaries, my father-in-law, Pietro Ettore Riola, was a student of languages, law, medicine and philosophy at the university. After graduating in 1899, he was sent on an extended tour of Europe and the Western Hemisphere, after which he was expected to settle down in a properly arranged marriage.

The scenario was set.

Fate changed all that. At a stopover in New York Harbor, Amelia DeCesare Valentino joined the other passengers, including Pietro. She was a young widow, barely 20, and much too young to sink into permanent mourning. To get her out among people again, her doctor had recommended a sea voyage.

You've guessed the end of this narrative, I'm sure.

Amelia and Pietro met aboard ship, immediately fell in love, and, by the time the leisurely voyage was over, were thinking in terms of marriage.

Of course, it wasn't as simple as that. Back in Naples, Pietro's family did not look favorably on his sudden wedding plans. Especially since this unknown bride-to-be was not of their choosing.

After much "serious consultation," it was decided that Pietro and the wife of his choice would make their home in the United States. His father agreed to finance him in a new business venture as a chemist.

The family honor was saved!

And that's the tale of the Americanization of this particular Riola family, a true love story with a happy ending.

Sara Hewitt Riola
Lakewood, New Jersey

The Barn Came Before the House

My great-grandfather utilized the opportunities available to him in his adopted country, as did many immigrants of his time. He came with nothing more than frugality, shrewdness, good health and the willingness to work hard.

Born December 22, 1842, near Schwarzenburg, Canton Bern, Switzerland, Christian Marti grew up on a small farmstead, *Heimigesslen.* In 1866 conscription papers were served on him. Christ undoubtedly begrudged the amount of money it took to equip himself with the 16 items necessary to fulfill his army obligations. In 1866 he indentured himself to the Widow Uhlmann for 500 francs—which he worked off by 1868. (We have these papers.) According to family oral tradition, he left his widowed mother, his brother and sisters, his homeland, and a familiar way of life and used the widow's francs to buy passage to America.

Family historians say that it was early on a chilly morning when Christ Marti arrived in St. Joseph, Missouri. Believing that he could find an inn along the railroad tracks as one did back in Switzerland, he began walking north. Finding no accommodations along the way, he walked to Amazonia to get his breakfast; he remained in the vicinity for the rest of his life. Some family members say that he arrived with less than $1 in his pocket and that he bought an axe instead of breakfast because he found work north of Amazonia with the Ent family. He worked for them the next three years.

By that time he had saved $100—which was enough to make a down payment on 40 acres, a log cabin with a shed kitchen and a shed barn. The total cost of this outlay was $1,000. About half the land was in timber.

After that, he needed a cook/housekeeper. In the German-speaking Swiss settlement around Amazonia resided the Christian Bachmann family from Goldivyl, Switzerland. Christian Marti and his future father- and brother-in-law filed "Intent to Declare Citizenship" papers simultaneously in December 1870.

The Bachmann family included three daughters of marrying age: Magdalena, Rosa and Anna. It was not determined during his first call on the family just which daughter Christ was interested in. But on the second visit, he brought a box of candy and presented it to Magdalena. They were married in Amazonia on February 11, 1872, and proceeded to the farm six miles northwest. Magdalena cried upon her arrival. Among other things, there was no gate on the fence around the yard. Her mother had also warned her not to wear her nice clothing from Chicago to church or to other outings. Her mother reasoned it would be more appropriate to come attired in a sunbonnet and calico dress as other women did.

Some neighbors and others, including his wife, surely thought Christ would build a house first, since five children had joined the family by the time he was ready to build. However, Christ justified his decision thusly, "No, ze barn will build ze house!"

Most of the lumber came from timber on the farm. Trees were cut and hauled to the sawmill. The framework, made of whole logs, was hewed by hand. All sections were marked with Roman numerals. When neighbors came to help with the barn-raising, the joints were all ready to be put into place. The famous "Marti" barn still stands sturdily on its rock foundation, its tree-length beams still held together with doweled and mitered joints instead of nails.

The children born in that first log home were: Rosa, 1872; John, 1874; Alfred Christian "Oliver," 1877; Ida Magdalena, my grandmother, 1879; and Emma Marie, 1880.

Then came the house building, which produced a structure neither as large nor as grand as many of the other local Swiss houses. Nevertheless, the house was adequate, with a finished cellar underneath, four rooms on the first floor and four above, with porches along the east and west sides. Born in the new home were two more daughters: Susanna Flora, 1884; and Minnie, 1886. I too was born in this house many years later—in 1930.

Much of the housework was done in the nearby rock cheese house, with a fireplace above, a cellar beneath, and a well for cooling nearby. Cheese making and milk care were performed there, as well as family washings and other tasks. This building is also standing up well, but the house has begun to deteriorate due to misuse, abuse and vandals.

The milking industry was important to the family income and consumed much of Magdalena's time and energy. When milk arrived at the stone cheese house, some was made into butter. A large part was made into cheese, which, after aging, Christ sold for 10 cents a pound in St. Joseph on his weekly trips. The whey was fed to the hogs. Christ also took whatever else was in season to sell, such as apples, potatoes and grapes.

Magdalena and Christian Marti's lives were not free from worry and hardship. Somehow, though, they managed to raise their seven children, to acquire 900 acres of debt-free land, to milk 30 cows, to raise hogs, and to produce crops of wheat, oats, corn and clover. The farmstead contained both table and "truck" gardens, an acre vineyard, and a 20-acre orchard—primarily apple.

The couple was generous. Daughters who wanted to were allowed to attend the Normal School at Stanberry. Emma found a teacher-husband there; Flora, a preacher. As each child married, he or she was given part of the land and/or inheritance money. Two half-orphan grandsons who had shared the Marti home were also gift recipients. Marti land was also passed to grandchildren, and Marti family members occupied that homestead for 80 years. It eventually passed from Marti hands in the late 1950s.

This Swiss great-grandfather of mine, Christian Marti, who walked from St. Joseph to Amazonia just to get his breakfast, traveled—with the aid of his wife—an even longer road to become a success and a credit to his adopted country.

Betty E. Nelson
Graham, Missouri

Temporarily Lost at Sea

My mother came from Switzerland in 1906, accompanying an uncle who had come to America years before. He went back to Switzerland to visit his sister, who was my mother's mother. There were four girls in the family, and there seemed to be no future for them there. He brought the two youngest girls to America. My mother was 15 and her sister was 17. The uncle and his wife ran a boarding house in Ohio, and he said my mother could go to school and her sister could help his wife in the boarding house.

On the way across the ocean their ship had engine trouble near a small island, where they had to wait for repairs. It took them four weeks to get to America. They had no way to notify Mother's family, so they were almost given up as lost. They finally got to Ellis Island, where they had to wait almost a week to get a physical before continuing their journey to Ohio. My mother lived with her uncle and family for four years. She then went to Iowa to visit her sister who had married and moved there.

While there she married my father. He and Mother's sister's husband were brothers, who came to Iowa from Switzerland in 1909.

In 1954 my parents were able to take a trip back to Switzerland to visit their relatives. I'm sure the plane trip was much more pleasant than that earlier trip to America by boat.

Esther Olson
Denison, Iowa

Family Called Experimental Community Home

My paternal grandfather, John Lindemulder, deserted the Dutch navy to come to America. His girlfriend, Kay Batema, later my grandmother, came with her parents to farm in Grand Rapids, Michigan. My grandfather came with them, declared that he had $20 and was a farmer, too. By the time I came along they had moved to a Dutch neighborhood on Chicago's South Side.

It was the practice at the time, in Holland at least, for the family to save money to send the oldest son to America. He would earn money at whatever job he could find and send it to bring the rest of his family to join him. I believe this was the case with all of my grandparents.

The older Batema and Lindemulder boys worked in a laundry in Grand Rapids.

My maternal grandfather, Sam Hoekstra, came with his family when he was 6 years old. His older brother was recruited in Holland by the Pullman Company, which built railroad cars south of Chicago. My grandfather also went to work for Pullman when he was 12 years old and worked there until he retired at 65.

My Grandpa Lindemulder also went to work at Pullman, but later went into the trucking business, hauling produce, smoked fish, Christmas trees, etc. from Michigan to the Chicago market.

My Grandma Hoekstra, neé Susan Vanderveen, was living in one of the Pullman homes for employees when she was orphaned. Grandpa Hoekstra met her through her brothers. I suspect it was an arranged marriage, as I know that Grandma ended up doing all the housework and laundry for both households. She was only 15.

The Pullman community was a self-contained city established by the company for its employees. At the time it was touted as a great social experiment. There were rows upon rows of adjoining brick two- and three-story houses. There were company-owned stores, a hotel, a hospital, schools, bars, recreation halls, gyms, dormitories for single men and anything else that might be needed. There was even a technical high school for the training of the next generation of workers. The community still stands today, with many of the buildings restored as historical landmarks.

Pullman sent representatives all over Europe to recruit workers. Their fare would be paid and they would get housing.

The factory was organized by nationalities. My grandparents, and most others of Dutch descent, worked in the woodworking shop where all the cabinets and wood trim were made. Other nationalities worked in separate shops. That way they could communicate with everyone in their work place. The housing was mixed, meaning your neighbors could be Irish, Polish or German. As a little girl, I was amazed that my grandfather, who had never gone past the sixth grade in school, could speak six languages.

Before I was born, the families had moved to the Chicago Dutch community of Roseland. The Lindemulders and the Hoekstras lived next door to each other. The families were very close. My parents, who were the same age, took short business courses after eighth grade and went to work. They never dated anyone else and married as soon as they reached the age of 21, when they did not need parental consent. My mother's sister married my father's brother.

Roseland was a community dominated by four Dutch Reformed Churches. The next community over was the Polish, and then there was a community of Irish, both with their bars, lodges, theaters and Catholic Churches. The Dutch section was dry. Movie going and joining a lodge were forbidden.

Eleanor Lindemulder Mattausch
Benson, Arizona

A Family Secret Revealed

My maternal grandmother was born in Switzerland. She had a baby boy before she was married. Leaving her baby with her parents, she came to America to start a new life. She soon married my grandfather, who also had immigrated from Switzerland. (I often wonder if they knew one another before they came to America. I'll never know, they have been gone for many years.)

They soon had a baby boy of their own. My grandparents then sent back to Switzerland and had my grandmother's first son sent over to live with them in America. My grandparents had seven more children, among them my mother.

It was not until many years later that they discovered their eldest brother was really a half-brother. My grandfather's brother, who still lived in Switzerland, died and left a small inheritance to be divided among his brother's children—except for the eldest son. So the story became known.

My paternal great-grandfather came to America from Germany along with a good friend. Later this friend's fiancée came over too. Great-Grandfather's friend had been killed in an accident, so he married his friend's fiancée. They had several children together. Several years ago my sister and I visited their graves in Arcadia, Iowa. If only they could have told us their story!

Clarice Morrison
Coleridge, Nebraska

Pride Keeps Culture Alive

In November of 1912, our mother, with her mother and two sisters, journeyed by ship, *The Martha Washington,* traveling 21 days across the ocean in search of a better life and prosperity. She was 12 at the time.

Her family had lived in a small town called Store, near the big city of Celje in Slovenija. At that time it was part of Yugoslavia; as of June 1991, it is independent. They went by train to Trieste, where they boarded *The Martha Washington* the following day. Mother said it was a huge ship, which was later sunk during World War I by the Germans. The passengers were all given physical exams before they were allowed to board. For awhile they enjoyed smooth sailing and a sunny sky, then suddenly it got cloudy. The wind began to blow and rock the vessel. Mother and one of her sisters who was on deck grabbed a pole so they wouldn't be swept into the ocean, as all the dishes and everything that was not attached were. The sailors came to their aid and took them to their room, where Grandmother and another aunt were in bed, seasick. The sailors closed the heavy windows, which made the room dark. When the storm subsided and the heavy windows were opened, they could see fish as large as oxen or buffalo, which were following the ship. Mother said they were afraid they might never see land again, so they were very happy when they saw the Statue of Liberty.

When they came to shore, they were told to watch for their trunk and possessions. When they claimed theirs, they were told to proceed. They rode on a small boat for a short while. When they reached land again they were taken to a railroad station in New York. There, for $1 each, Grandmother bought boxes containing salami, cheese, canned meat, bread, fruit, oranges, apples and bananas. They had never seen a banana before and were not sure they were edible. By then they were getting tired but still had a long journey ahead.

They rode the train from New York to St. Louis, where they transferred for the rest of their trip. Their destination was Breezy Hill, Kansas, a small settlement where immigrants came to live near Mulberry, Kansas. At the Mulberry station a man with a horse-drawn wagon was waiting to take them to their home. Grand-father and my uncle were already in America, having come a few years earlier to find employment and a place for the family to live.

My father came from Slovenija to Breezy Hill, too, where his sister and family lived. Our mom worked as a cook at the boarding house where the men without families lived. This was a coal mining area. Mom and Dad became acquainted and were married in 1917. They borrowed the money for three acres of ground in Camp 50, Girard, Kansas. There they built the home where my two sisters and I were born. It cost them $800 to have the new four-room home built, complete with pantry and clothes closet. There was no elec-tricity in the area until later. They had a cow, two pigs and a good number of chickens. They worked hard in the garden to grow a lot of vegetables, which Mother would can in preparation for the win-ter. With no refrigerators, our mother and the neighborhood women had to prepare everything at the time it was needed. Mother was a good seamstress and made all of our clothes, as well as all the beautiful handiworks: embroidery, knitting, and crocheting, which she did after the rest of her day's work was done.

This was considered a melting pot. People of all nationalities were our neighbors: French, Belgians, Germans, Poles and Italians. Our community was called Camp 50; most of the settlements were named after the numbered coal mine nearest them. The language barrier was a problem but somehow the people seemed to understand one another. Mom and Dad attended adult education classes and learned a lot. They both became naturalized citizens of the United States, and we were very proud of them. I attended classes at the night school because I was afraid to stay at home alone in the evenings. The night school teacher gave me a group of people to teach English to, and when they understood the language, they were promoted to his class, where he taught the Constitution and government.

Through the years, my parents kept in touch with their relatives and friends in Slovenija. They taught us the Slovene language: how to converse, read and write. My sisters and I still keep in touch with our people in Slovenija.

We went to Slovenija to meet and visit with our relatives and friends with whom we had been corresponding. We were greeted and treated with such love and hospitality, we can now say, "We know how it must feel to be a queen."

Mom and Dad worked hard for what they received. They didn't ask for a handout, only for the opportunity and privilege to work for a living. Dad was a coal miner for more than 40 years. On his knees, underground, he risked his life for $2 a day, but not every day, as there was not such a demand for coal. He was handy with wood carving and made scythe handles and wooden rakes completely by hand. The men used scythes in those days as there were no lawn mowers.

The coal miners in the area went on strike in 1921 for better working conditions and better pay. Mother was with the group of ladies who marched to try to keep the non-union men—called scabs—from going down in the mine to work. The men stayed at home and took care of the children, as the leaders thought there would be less trouble if the ladies marched.

There are 35 second-generation Slovenes in our singing group called Zivio Slovenci. We march in parades, attend homecomings and sing for special events. These are the same songs our parents sang. Visiting and singing the songs from their homeland was their recreation. We are trying to keep the culture and language alive in this area; we are proud of our Slovenian ancestry.

Angeline M. O'Korn
Girard, Kansas

Little Straw Huts on the Prairie

The Weeda and De Booy families lived in Alsace-Lorain near France, but they spoke Dutch.

In 1852, several families from that area decided to come to America. They sailed to New Orleans, then up the Mississippi River to Keokuk, Iowa. After unloading their stock and furnishings, they stayed with other Holland people nearby. The men and older boys set out to scout the country for a place to settle and make their new home. They followed the Des Moines River in a northwestern direction. Some of the men found just the place they wanted and returned to Keokuk to get their families.

The Weeda and De Booy group continued on until they came to a location that they thought was paradise. The land—between the Skunk and Des Moines Rivers—was level and the soil very fertile. The town was called "Strawtown" because there were so many straw hut dwellings. The huts were made from prairie grass. They could purchase the virgin acres at a going price of $1.25 per acre. Upon their arrival they began to establish new homes. They hired-out to farmers and merchants and also rented ground for large gardens.

A 12-year-old boy named Cornelius De Booy, born in 1840, and a 10-year-old girl named Johanna Weeda, born in 1842, became close friends and later married. They lived in Pella, Iowa. To this union were born seven daughters and two sons. The younger son was my dad, Ira George De Booy, born in Pella, Iowa, in 1882.

Elizabeth Mae De Booy Malone
Stanton, California

Family Dissolved in the Great Melting Pot

My great-grandparents, Simon and Catherine Zeltner, immigrated to America in 1884 with their four children. They came from the Canton of Solothurn in Switzerland. According to my father, Simon did well for himself in Switzerland. He was a weaver and owned a silk factory. In addition, he brewed quantities of wine and whiskey for sale. Economics was not the factor influencing his coming to America. My father recalled that as a child he heard his grandfather speak of "the fever." In the 1880s an immigration fever apparently swept much of Europe. Simon was caught up in this desire to come to the new frontiers of America. In addition, Simon did not want his sons to be drafted into the Swiss military service.

My Great-Grandmother Catherine did not "catch" the immigration fever. She fought against coming to America, engaging in tears and tantrums in Switzerland before the trip; she continued her emotional binges in America. She was never happy here, and she refused to learn the language. Her grandchildren considered her disagreeable.

Simon had at least two brothers. John came to America some years before Simon and settled in St. Joseph, Missouri. He was a mason, hauling sand and rock from the Missouri River. The other brother went to the state of Washington and owned land where the city of Seattle was built. He made a fortune selling off his land and became a hero to the family because he was rich. My father heard about him constantly during his childhood but never saw him; he did not come to Missouri and Kansas to visit his poor relatives.

When I was a child, my Grandfather Gus told me many times of the sea voyage from Le Havre. Once, standing on deck, his new hat blew off and floated over the waves while he helplessly watched. The family feared Ellis Island. They worried that some unknown health problem would prevent their entering the country. These fears were unnecessary, as they were a hardy bunch.

After the family cleared Ellis Island, they were assigned a guide who spoke German. This guide accompanied them to New York and on the immigrant train west, never leaving them until they reached St. Joseph, Missouri. They "wintered" with the John Zeltner family. In the spring the family moved to a farm in Doniphan County, Kansas, and lived happily ever after—more or less. Everyone concentrated on learning the language, except contrary Catherine. For six months they all went to school to learn English. They must have worked diligently because my Grandfather Gus spoke without a European accent.

It seems strange to me, but apparently the Simon Zeltner family came to America and never looked back. They dissolved in the great melting pot. My father could not remember that they maintained any sustained correspondence or ties with Switzerland. They never exhibited any desire to return for a visit. My grandfather once told me that when they saw the flat, fertile land of Kansas, it was a love affair at first sight. Even after the Great Depression, when Gus could have afforded to travel, he told me he had no desire to return. Perhaps they were intoxicated with America's freedoms. Who really knows what visions danced in their heads.

Bernice Zeltner Rounds

Severance, Kansas

Faith Carried Family Through Adversities

My grandmother's family emigrated from the Netherlands in 1919, arriving in the United States on November 19. They settled on a farm near Boyden, Iowa. Grandmother immigrated at age 11 with her father, mother, two brothers and one sister because her father wanted to go to *"mooce Amerika"* the land of prosperity, where money was plentiful and there was always lots of food to eat. They also sought more freedoms, since the Netherlands government had many controls on farming operations after World War I. But how different they found life here.

Grandmother came aboard *The New Amsterdam,* traveling third class even though her family had purchased second-class passages. Each day Grandmother would walk over the decks of the ship with her father to get fresh air; they were the only family members who did not suffer seasickness. Grandmother ate many salted crackers, which were given to help against seasickness. She remembers eagerly watching to see the Statue of Liberty as their ship entered New York Harbor. After their family was processed through Ellis Island they went to a mainland hotel. Grandmother says it seemed as if the people were saying "yib yib yib," as she did not understand English. When their immigrating group entered the hotel, one man fell against a window, breaking it. After much difficulty it was understood that they did not have to pay damages.

Grandmother traveled from New York to Chicago by train. Their family was detained in Chicago. They huddled together, lying against each other to rest on the train depot bench, with their few trunks of belongings at their feet. Grandmother remembers many people stopping to look at them and shaking their heads as they walked away. Her family continued by train to the farm community of Boyden, Iowa, where they lived with relatives. They were gladdened with the birth of a baby girl two months after they arrived.

Grandmother was placed several grades back in school to the third grade because she was unable to speak English. When she tried to say something the other students laughed. Grandmother became determined not to say another word until she learned the new language well. She sat in school without saying a word for one whole year.

In the spring of 1920 Grandmother's family moved to their own rented 40-acre farm. One neighbor farm lady helped the family by baking all their bread from large sacks of flour they took her. It was Grandmother's job to bring home fresh-baked loaves for her mother.

Grandmother often said, "Oh! Had we but stayed in the Netherlands." Her family did not like the cold weather, deep snow and sticky mud in America. But Grandmother's family made the best of it as their mother taught them to do. Grandmother continued in school until she could speak the new language well, which earned her the responsibility of helping her father with his farm business. Grandmother occasionally worked as a hired girl for $1 a day until marrying my grandfather in the summer of 1929. My grandparents farmed together through many hardships and shared each other's happiness until Grandfather's death in the summer of 1972. Grandmother, now 85, lives comfortably with her youngest son in her own home in Inwood, Iowa, living on the income from two quarter sections of farmland she owns. Their faith in God carried them through their many adversities in this new land.

Brenda Fluit
Inwood, Iowa

Shoemaker Realized Dream of Land Ownership

Grandpa often wished he was a landowner like his brother-in-law, Giuseppe Spera. His prosperous olive and lemon groves allowed him to work in the fresh air and sunshine, and during slack time, he fished in the Gulf of Castellammare. But Grandpa was a shoemaker. He was always too busy for leisure time.

During family gatherings, he heard repetitious stories of the horrors of war and uprisings. His forefathers had fled Greece because of the barbarous Turks. Now, Grandpa faced the heavy taxes that had been levied in Italy for 100 years to support the military.

He wanted to raise his family free from heavy taxation and wars, and he still dreamed of being a landowner.

One day, Grandpa received a letter from his cousin in America. Cousin Luigi said free land was available in Nebraska by fulfilling six months of residency and farming the land. Grandpa had no knowledge of farming but could learn for the privilege of land ownership. Just think! Free land!

Grandma was not so excited, but consented to the move. They agreed that Grandma would remain there with Rosie, the oldest child, until Grandpa could file on some land.

Disposing of his business, he booked passage on a merchant vessel to America, landing at Ellis Island, New York, in February of 1888. Because of the language barrier and not knowing where to go, he began walking down the street. A kind woman called from her window in Italian, "You must be freezing in those light clothes; come in and have coffee and a sandwich!" Hearing his plight, she referred him to a bachelor friend, who offered him shelter in his apartment. Grandpa slept on the floor on his first night in America.

Arriving in Nebraska, he learned the free land was gone! By this time, Grandma was already on her way with 4-year-old Rosie and 4-month-old Mary, so he rented a shop on 13th and Jones Street and opened a shoe shop in Omaha, Nebraska.

When Grandma and the girls arrived, she related the excitement of crossing the Atlantic ocean—how Rosie refused to eat and how the ship's cook would favor her with fresh biscuits and jelly. She marveled at the fascinating gas lights in New York and seeing her first bananas ever! Grandpa then related how everybody wanted their shoes repaired, rather than purchasing new ones, and they all wanted boots! This was rural America.

Living in cramped quarters in the back of the shop, they began to learn the new language, mostly from food products and kind neighbors.

Five years later, Cousin Luigi informed Grandpa that several homesteaders, who were his neighbors, were discouraged and wanted to sell. Grandpa quickly bargained for their land in Custer County and moved his family to a small frame house with no foundation, consisting of a kitchen, pantry, sitting room and one small bedroom. This building was later used for a schoolhouse. Grandpa then opened a shoe shop in Anselmo, farming the land until my father and his brother were old enough to work it.

My grandfather realized his dream of land ownership and blessed his descendants with American citizenship. What a privilege!

Joseph F. Lepant
Grand Island, Nebraska

Distant Relatives May Be Relocated

My dad's family originated in Normandy, France. From there they migrated to England, where they shortened their name from "du Jeanes" to the simpler form "Janes."

The first of my ancestors, William Janes, came to America in 1637. Settling in Connecticut, he continued to be a schoolteacher.

By the early 1700s, several of my ancestors had left Connecticut and settled in Pennsylvania. Among these was a man also named William Janes, his wife, Hannah, and their three children, a 12-year-old girl, a 7-year-old boy, and a new baby son.

One day when William was away getting supplies, Indians attacked his family. When he returned, he found all three children dead. The two oldest had been scalped, the baby dashed against a tree. Hannah, also scalped, had been left for dead. Amazingly, she survived and bore her husband four more children.

Now, after nearly 300 years, my husband and I are anticipating a trip to France. Thanks to help from French friends—whom we talk with regularly via amateur radio—and my husband's ability to speak a little of the language, the possibility of being able to locate some of my distant relatives is exciting.

Mary M. Meyers
Aurora, Missouri

Family Spread from Coast to Coast

My Grandfather Vellios first came to the United States as a stowaway. We were told he came several more times by working on ships.

Grandfather and his two brothers envisioned a better life in this country than in their homeland, Greece. It was on Grandfather's fifth trip that he and his brothers came to Ellis Island for processing. He was just 17.

One brother did not pass the physical and returned to Greece. The other became successful in the restaurant business in the East. My grandfather went to work for the railroad. Along the way he met a pretty French girl who became my grandmother.

Life was hard in some ways and rewarding in others. Just recently I learned that my grandfather never drove—never had a car—and they all walked a lot. My grandfather died on his job.

A really memorable thing is my Uncle Bob's cooking. My mom and I suspect Bob got his great cooking skills from his dad and uncles. I wish I could share a recipe here but my uncle, Bob Vellios, always said it was a secret. All I can tell you is that I think his skills are a combination of effort and inheritance.

In the 74 years since Grandfather immigrated, his family has spread from coast to coast. I think he would be quite surprised.

Jerry Miller
Huffman, Texas

A Joyful Family Reunion

About 1912, my father, Joe Miceli, left Sicily, Italy, and came with his mother and a younger brother, Sam, to New York City. The young men had been working in a sulfur mine—a filthy, dangerous place to work.

"When I was about 6 years of age," he later told me, "your mother, Mary, who was my cousin, took a tomato can, added a few beans and gave it to me. This custom was regarded as a sign that she would be my sweetheart and we would someday be married. She and I sent letters back and forth across the ocean."

When Mary was 12, she and her mother, Rosa Rombola, along with two older sisters, Sadie and Millie, and a brother came to New York City and made their home with father's family, the Micelis.

Mary was large for her age and found a job in a laundry. Shortly after that Joe and Mary were married.

"A few months later, my wife, Mary, gave birth to you and your twin, Joseph," Father explained. "Because she was not given the proper care and enough food, she and your brother died.

"I tried to make a home for you, but I was drafted into the United States Army and sent to France. I left without seeing you because you were with your mother's family—the Rombolas. They too were very poor and had several small children. One more mouth to feed was not exactly what they needed.

"Soon you became very ill and had to be taken to Bellevue Hospital. Your grandmother went to visit you as often as she could but because she could not even afford the nickel for the car fare, it was necessary to place you in a foundling home.

"I was sitting in a Red Cross shelter drinking coffee some-where in France a few weeks before the Armistice was signed. A letter came from your grandmother telling me that she could not take care of you any longer and that the nurses told her you had been taken to a foundling home. They told her that as soon as I came home from the war they would help me trace you.

"Two years later I was discharged. The first place I went to was the institution. They told me how sorry they were, but a mistake had been made in the records. You had been adopted and they could not tell me where you were. I was furious. I lost my head and was arrested for disturbing the peace. From that time on I searched. I wrote letters—hundreds of them. I begged newspapers to publish articles in which pictures of my daughter could be printed. Some of them did, and I will show them to you. I wrote to Fiorello La Guardia, also called "The Little Flower." At that time he was serving in the United States House of Representatives. Later he became famous as the mayor of New York City.

"I wrote to Eleanor Roosevelt. She answered personally to tell me how sorry she was, but there was nothing she could do. Then I picketed the mayor's office and was carried off to jail.

"I continued my search and spent a great deal of money hiring lawyers and detectives. I went to court several times and always the case was dismissed. Because of my frustrations and the actions that resulted I was sent to a mental institution for six months. From there I wrote to Al Capone, my countryman, but received no reply.

"By then I had remarried and had several children. A judge reminded me that I was having difficulty raising my family. He asked me why I wanted the other child. I told him that if he lost his dog, he would have 100 police out looking for it, but because I lost my daughter while fighting for this country, you call me crazy and want to lock me up.

"A month ago a man came into my cigar store. He bought 10 boxes of hand-rolled cigars. On the same day he returned and purchased 15 more boxes. The next day he came in for 20 more boxes and told me that he was a private detective. I gave him $100 and asked him to have a doctor at the New York Foundling Home sign a paper so I could look at my daughter's records. I received a letter from the foundling home. They said that they knew where Mary was. She was well, but that was all they could tell me. However, they would write to her and give her a chance to contact me.

"Two weeks later you called your grandmother. She said they didn't have a daughter named Mary. You were very excited and told them you lived in Ohio, but didn't give them your address or telephone number.

"Two days before this happened, my youngest brother, your Uncle Sam, died. I had closed my store out of respect, but I went over to check my mail. Your grandfather, Angelo Rombola, was there. He offered me a chair and said, 'Joe, your daughter called today. She is coming here to see you.' My heart went up like a broomstick.

"Three days later I received a letter from you. There were pictures of you and your husband. I was so excited I didn't know what I was doing. I bought a few bottles of wine and gave a drink to all my friends with a little special whiskey for me. I closed the store and took a cab to Grand Central Station. I didn't even take time to change my work clothes. I bought a ticket for the first train to Toledo, Ohio. The train was one hour late. I didn't know what to do. I bought a few drinks at the station.

"At 11:00 p.m., we finally left New York City. At 1:00 p.m. we arrived in Toledo. Should I take a taxi? No, I wouldn't want to surprise her and make her sick. I called from the phone at the depot. Your husband answered.

"Who is calling?"

"Mary's father."

"How are you and your family?"

"They are all fine. I am in Toledo. I just got off the train."

"Stay where you are. I'll be right down to get you."

"Will you know me if you see me?"

"Yes, I think so, because last night I saw your picture."

"Where is my daughter?"

"She went to church but will be home very soon, probably before we get there."

"When we arrived at the house you were there. You nodded to your husband and then you saw me. You said, 'This is my father.'

"I was so happy. I told you to call your grandfather and my sister, Racial, who is your godmother. Racial asked where I was. She said that they were holding Sunday dinner for me. I heard you proudly say, 'He is here in Toledo with me, his daughter.'"

The Friday morning after Thanksgiving we arrived in a snowy New York City. Already the stores were raising the heavy black gates to display their wares. Trucks were unloading racks of clothing, which were being rolled into the stores. Street vendors were arranging fruits and other groceries in stalls.

My husband, father, foster-mother, Sarah, and I were en route on the dirty streets of Manhattan by taxicab. I relived the long night on the train. Dim lights overhead created phantomlike figures that silently moved in the aisle. Once my father woke me as he gently placed a fresh pillow under my head.

About 2:30 a.m. I made my way down the perilous darkened aisle, dodging limbs here and there that extended from sleepy passengers attempting to obtain some kind of rest. When I entered the dingy, tiny cubicle of a bathroom, I sat on a short stool and surveyed myself in the cracked mirror. "What are you doing here?" I asked myself. "What do you know about this man and the people where you are going? Will they accept you?"

We alighted from the cab in the shadow of the Triborough Bridge. My father paid the driver. He directed us to a basement apartment on 123rd Street. He signaled me to ring the bell. A lady about my age opened the door. I stepped back. I felt that I was looking at myself.

"My God, it is Mary. Come in. All of you, come in."

My father said, "This is my daughter, Mary, and here, Mary, is your mother's sister, Sadie. Here are your mama's mother and father, Sadie and Angelo Rombola." He then introduced them to my husband, Fred, and my foster-mother, Sarah.

I soon realized that the doubts that had assaulted me in the rest room on the train were unfounded. I was accepted and so was my family from Toledo.

Over mugs of steaming coffee, stories were exchanged. My mother, Sarah, cried as she listened to my grandmother tell how the family had been separated from her dead daughter's child. On another table a jug of grape wine was being dispatched by the menfolk.

White-haired Grandfather Rombola, supporting himself with a cane, told of the countless times he had accompanied his son-in-law, Joseph, to the authorities and the orphanage. He described visits to the mental hospital where Joe had been sent more than once when he was unable to control himself.

Sadie was overjoyed. She said that she had found another "sister" in me. "I must call your Aunt Millie and the others," she said, and immediately took up the phone inviting all the family to "come and see Mary." Grandma prepared breakfast for all of us. French toast covered with powdered sugar, tall glasses of milk and several kinds of fruit were consumed.

After breakfast, Grandma and Sadie began the preparations for dinner. There would, of course, be meatballs with spaghetti. Grandpa was sent out to purchase the meat and more fruit. This was before Vatican II, when meat on Fridays was forbidden. But in all the excitement nobody remembered, and who could blame them? During the preparations my father filled gaps in the wondrous story with vivid episodes from the past.

It wasn't long before Sadie's sister, Millie, arrived with her husband, Charlie. Again more tears and embraces. She was also in her early 40s.

Aunt Millie's son and his wife arrived, followed by more cousins and neighbors. Coffee and fruits were offered, and soon the small kitchen was crowded. The jug of red wine was on the table without a cork. By that time some members from my father's side (Miceli) of the family had arrived. They too were very happy for my father and his daughter. My godmother was excited and said, "Now we'll see Joe smile again."

It was decided to rent a hall and invite everyone who wanted to share the good luck. On Saturday evening, more relatives and friends gathered, some with gifts, all with good will, pasta, cakes, Italian cookies and wine to share.

Our visit lasted three days, with people coming each day. Finally, late Sunday night, my husband and mother left with me. We were laden with gifts and good wishes for our home in Toledo, Ohio.

My father came to the train with us, and the last glimpse I had of him was a smiling face mouthing the words, "I'll come and visit you soon." When I went to the rest room on that home-bound trip, my heart was much lighter; I realized that the reunion was a long-awaited answer to my prayers.

Mary Bowermaster
Sarasota, Florida

Immigrant Helped Himself and Others

Grandfather Christian Schultz was born March 11, 1842, in Karlsberg, Russia. Forced to go to work early in life to supplement the family's income, he had only one month of schooling. At 15, Christian left home and went to South Russia, where he worked on a farm for two years. The next three years he apprenticed himself to a manufacturer. Here he learned to be a blacksmith and carriage maker. For three years he received only his board, then he began to earn wages. After 12 years, he was the best workman and the best paid on this job. During this time, he built a carriage that won first place at the World's Fair in St. Petersburg, Russia, in 1871.

Christian Schultz came to America on the *SS Frisia*, which departed from Hamburg, arriving in New York on July 22, 1874. He left during what became known as the "The Great Migration of the Germans from Russia," although we are neither German nor Russian, as our ancestors came from the Netherlands.

From New York, Christian came to Barton County, Kansas, where he settled with other immigrants in the colony at Dundee. This colony of people had been neighbors in the area of Christian's birthplace. Christian, who was 33, had saved about $3,000, which he used to buy a quarter section of land for this colony. Christian helped others who were less fortunate than him build their homes. He built a house for a widow—who later became his mother-in-law—and her seven children. The Santa Fe Railroad shipped the lumber free of freight charges from Michigan to Dundee. The approximate cost of lumber for each house was $40.35. The cost of lumber for beds, tables, benches, fuel boxes and shelves was $15.65 per 1,000 feet. Stoves were $25 each.

Christian saw to it that a stone church was built for this colony. In it, Christian and his bride, Helena Rudiger, were married September 5, 1875. When this colony disbanded after several years, the families began to buy land and settle down on larger farms. My grandparents, Christian and Helena, moved to farm an area north of Pawnee Rock, Kansas. Their first home was a dugout, in which their first four children were born. Then Grandfather built a log house, where the rest of his children were born. They had 14 children, two of whom died shortly after birth.

My mother, Eva, was their second daughter. She often told how busy she and the oldest daughter were helping their mother with this big family. Christian built a lovely new two-story house for his family in 1905. My mother married November 7, 1900, so she did not get to enjoy living in this new home, but she and her husband enjoyed coming "home" to visit her parents.

My parents, Eva and Sam Boese, raised their children on the farm, where they used horses for everything. They pulled the farming machinery, the wagon that took us across country to church, and a buggy that took us to our country school.

I'm glad my grandparents came to America and that I was born here. If it hadn't been for them, I wouldn't be enjoying America today.

Marjorie Andrasek
Garden City, Kansas

Settler Warned of Immigration Pros and Cons

Alto, Wisconsin
June 14, 1866

Dear Brothers and Sisters:

We want to let you know that we, through God's goodness, now are in good health, and hope we may hear the same of you.

We had a very difficult trip, which you perhaps know. All this was not what we had intended to subject our children to. The loss of our two children I can not forget, that will always stay with me and be a sharp thorn in my flesh. This has taken all our pleasure and enjoyment. If God did not give me the power and strength, then I would collapse. It is impossible to describe how hard this has been for us. Those of you who have children can almost imagine what we all are going through.

As to our state of affairs we have rented a log house after we had been here for 14 days and we are living in it now. We have five hectares (about 12 acres) of arable land, just like it is over there. We rent the land for $40. We bought two milk cows for $57 for the two. We have some for our use and sell 50 cents worth of milk every week. There are places we can buy here, which were offered to us almost before we got here. One place of 80 acres near Rediker, with a good house on it, we could buy for $72, but I did not dare risk it because I knew nothing about conditions here, so we just rented this small place instead. This way, we won't have the chance to gain anything, but we don't have to lose, either. If we find something better later, we can always leave here. In the fall they tell me one can rent larger places, and I'd rather start on a small scale and not go into debt. You can imagine that it sounds good to buy such a large place, but everything you need to buy for such a place is very expensive. Things are done *quite differently here than in Holland. It's all done with machinery. It is easier to earn a dollar a day here than to earn four stuvers (20 cents) in Holland. Food costs are expensive here. We buy meat for 7 cents a pound, the best pork is 12 cents. Wheat meal is 3 1/2 cents, buckwheat is 2 1/2 cents a pound. Everything is according to American pennies. The way it seems I cannot notice things are much different here than they are in Holland. If I didn't know how long the trip was coming out here, I would not be able to believe that we were such a distance apart.*

The area around here is particularly nice, and we are enjoying ourselves exceptionally well. The children are attending the American school. In the summer they are starting a new school sponsored by the church.

The people are very friendly and helpful and come to visit us every day. Before we had our own cows or anything else, they provided us with everything. Everyone said, "Feel free to come if there is anything you need."

When it comes to religion and worship, it is much like in Holland. We never get into a home where the Bible is not read and audible blessings and thanks are not said at every meal. On Sunday they are very strict to have all business places closed, and they would rather not speak about world problems. I do not know if they are sincere because I don't know their hearts, yet I find it particularly edifying.

A lot of Hollanders are living in these surroundings with few Americans, several of which are leaving and are glad to sell their farms. Yet there are many coming with money who will get along all right. Many who come without money find it isn't anything like they expected.

The young men who came with us are rather disappointed. Jan Van Den Berg had written about a man earning $200 a year, but farmers here pay $100, and anyone who is slow will find it difficult to find a farmer who will hire him. In Holland people often spoke of farmers being able to pay good wages but I can give you a little hint. Everything here is done by machinery and horses such as sowing, mowing and threshing. Not too much work is done to the land. The land that grew wheat last year and had been mowed was still a stubble field when we came in April. They plow the fields before they sow wheat. The corn and potatoes are not planted until a week or two before the first of May. The land is plowed and the corn and potatoes planted. I have thought and said if we worked the land in Holland this way we wouldn't get anything. The straw is put on piles and burned. That is what is done with the wood. The bigger branches are sawed and used for fuel in stoves and the twigs are burned.

How often I think if only the things that are burned here were in Holland. Oh, how many poor souls out there have to go to the woods with a sack and gather twigs. Here it is burned or they let it rot. I believe if people here would work the land the way it is done in Holland they would reap a lot more. Anyone here who works 80 acres of land can easily work the land with the help of one hired man, except in the busy season, when they sometimes pay someone $2 a day. On a farm like this they can harvest about 800 bushels of wheat if they grow 40 acres, and they have corn, potatoes, and hay and a pasture for their cattle. They do not keep many cows, mostly five or six, that is cows and calves and two horses. Wheat is about a dollar a bushel, and then you have $800, but you have to keep some to sow the following year, which is about a bushel and a half, and you have to keep some to eat. You can understand and figure what is left over. For those who have a good start, it is exceptionally good here, but those who come with little or no money, it takes some time to get a good start.

Thus, brothers and sisters, at the moment I cannot recommend too strongly and tell you to come, even if it would be so pleasant to have you here. I must first have more experience here, and if later we are more familiar with conditions, then I will write you more in detail.

Tell Arend Brink that Hendrick is still with us, and that he is enjoying himself and is well. He goes out working and is earning a dollar a day.

Greet everyone from me. There are too many to mention names. Write soon and let us know if all are well. Also how the business with hayland has gone.

I remain respectfully your brother,
Rijk Sneller
Submitted by Sandra Sumner
Dawson, Minnesota

Proud of Family's "Strong Stock"

My family came to the Land of Opportunity from France to escape the religious persecution of King Louis XIV. In 1685 he decided to rid France of all religions except Roman Catholicism. He issued the revocation of the "Edict of Nantes," in which he ordered all ministers to either revert to Catholicism, leave or be put to death. He gave them two weeks to comply, and ordered all churches and temples destroyed. He also ordered all other Protestants to stay.

In spite of the order to stay, a large group of John Calvin's followers, known as Huguenots, left France. Upwards of two million would leave France for destinations around the world. My immigrant ancestor was one of those who left and went to England, where he met and married his wife, then left for America. They arrived in New York in 1700, where their first two sons were born. They subsequently moved on to a large area of land set aside for them in Virginia. It was a deserted Indian village on the James River near Richmond. Manakin, Virginia, is the site of the Huguenot Church and cemetery marked by Virginia historical sign number 033. The church is still in the design of the original French church.

This immigrant would become wealthy and prominent in the area and the state, with much land and many slaves. His sons would continue to spread across the state and into Kentucky; they would also be wealthy. His grandsons helped carry on and finance the War of 1812.

The fourth and fifth generations of these new Americans would leave Kentucky, cross the mountains, and travel the Ohio, Mississippi, Missouri, and Osage Rivers. They would trek overland to get to the part of Missouri where many of them would remain. They did not leave the Civil War behind them; several of the men joined the Missouri Infantry and fought for their rights.

My great-grandmother, part of the family's sixth generation, would marry a young man who had just arrived from Kentucky.

He, his folks and brothers had come to take part in the Cherokee Strip Land Rush on September 16, 1893. They settled in northeast Oklahoma and would have eight children before he died in 1912. Two of the children had died, and she was with child when he —while saving an Indian friend—was dragged to his death by a team of spooked horses. At 36, she was a widow with a large family to raise.

She would have many more trials and tribulations and see sons and grandsons in more wars before her death. She was a very colorful lady who collected rattles from rattlesnakes, used snuff, and lived by "Tulsey" time until the day she died. She went to sleep in her favorite chair at her oldest daughter's home, and hopefully awoke in a better world than the one she left. There were five living generations of her family when she died in 1961. Fourteen generations are now recorded, and she left 305 direct descendants. I'm glad I came from such strong stock; they were certainly brave folks who followed their convictions.

Louise Parks
Bellflower, Missouri

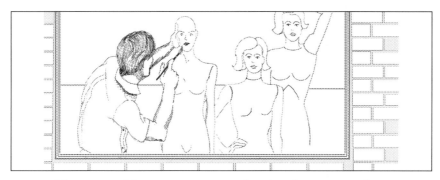

Chapter Six: Ancestors from the Americas

Painting Lips Kept American Dream Alive

On board the plane I felt like singing, and I honestly laughed when the cute stewardess served me salad, because I had never seen peaches in salad and thought that was so funny!

My heart was bursting with anticipation; I wanted to push the plane to go faster. When we finally arrived in Idlewild, New York, I thanked the Creator with all my heart for the great privilege. I still had to pinch myself to realize that I was not dreaming.

A taxi took me to a Manhattan hotel near the United Nations building. The driver asked me my name as I pointed out the wonders of the city. Just by coincidence, six months later I took the same taxicab. The driver remembered my name and said that my enthusiasm made him realize what a privilege it was to be an American.

I was so excited to be in New York. I started to walk down the streets—I walked and walked for two consecutive days without sleeping. Everything was new and wonderful: the people, the stores, the windows, Radio City, the Rockefeller Center ... I could not believe the amount of magazines and newspapers in some of the stands. I decided to buy the entire bunch and send them to my parents, because I thought that if I told them how many there were, they would have thought that I was exaggerating. I sent the huge package by ship.

Soon I was assigned to my position in the United Nations. They said that they wanted to introduce me to Latin American people, but I said I did not want to meet Latin Americans, I want to meet Americans. I did meet Joan Crawford. She looked so old in person but she was extra nice; she gave me a large autographed photo of her glamorous self.

Besides my assignment, I worked for radio programs, transcribing and acting in different episodes, including the one that I had written, "Citizens of the World."

I lived on Second Avenue, just a few blocks from my employment. It was a rooming house, but I thought it was a palace! The landladies, two Swedish sisters, were former maids of dancer-actor Ray Bolger.

I used to have breakfast at a coffee shop opposite my house. Everybody there became very friendly with me, so I felt as though I was with a new family.

One early morning, as I was getting ready to go for breakfast, a very familiar face looked at me. I though she was a relative or something because she looked so familiar. It was Miss Greta Garbo! She crossed the street and went into the same coffee shop that I used to go to, and I followed her like a puppy. When she went inside a phone booth I asked the manager to introduce me to her. He said definitely not—Miss Garbo did not want to be bothered by anyone. My pleas were completely ignored.

When Miss Garbo came out of the booth, I approached her and asked if she was Miss Garbo. She responded affirmatively. I introduced myself, saying, "My name is Ralph Campo and I am from Argentina!"

"Oh how interesting," she said, "I always wanted to go to Argentina!" I invited her to breakfast and she accepted. We talked about everything. She was extremely interested in hearing about Eva Perón, and she stayed with me for more than an hour. At the end of our conversation I said, "May I kiss your hand?" She responded, "Why don't you kiss my cheek instead?" My face turned tomato red. Since I was a little boy, I had admired Miss

Garbo; she was the epitome of everything imaginable, and there I was in America, kissing her! As soon as I got home, I wrote an eight-page letter to my mother describing every single little detail about that meeting. It was heaven to me!

A few months later the UN assigned me to Palestine, but I did not want to leave the United States. I was determined to stay here! Go or resign was the ultimatum, so I resigned. I had a diplomatic-type passport and visa that only allowed me to stay in the States 30 days longer.

I mentioned my predicament at the coffee shop, and all the customers pitched in to help me, placing an envelope in my hand with $300 and the address of immigration attorney Ira Ehrlich, who would help me get my immigration visa. After a couple of days of instructions, he said that I must visit the American Consulate in New Laredo, Mexico, where I could obtain my proper visa. I got a plane ticket to Dallas, Texas, taking a bus from there to my destination.

After a week of crossing the bridge daily from Laredo, Texas, to Nueva Laredo, Mexico, I finally obtained the consular visa. When I tried to return to the United States, a Mexican official told me that since I had not reported that I was there trying to get my visa, I was in Mexico illegally. He took my wallet and all but $10 of my money, then let me cross the bridge just a few minutes before US Customs closing time at 6:00 p.m.

I ran across the bridge, and as soon as I arrived in the United States I fell on my knees and kissed the soil, thanking God for getting my papers in order and giving me this new, proper chance.

I had to pay $8.50 for the fiscal stamp, so I was left with only $1.50. I did not want to call my parents at home and alarm them, so I went to a hotel, where I took a bath and prayed for a solution. I had a vivid, divine dream that I must buy a red tube of paint and a small brush. In the morning I went to Woolworth's, where I had coffee and a doughnut and bought a tube of bright red paint and a paintbrush.

As I left the store, I noticed a large department store with a lot of mannequins, all of which had faded lips due to the strong sun. With my broken English, I insisted on talking to the manager of the store. I took him outside to show him the discolored lips on all the mannequins, and I said to him, "I'll paint them for 10 cents per lip." He said, "OK!" I started to paint lips, lips and more lips ... At the end of the day I had painted more than 300. While I was painting the lips on one mannequin, a man knocked on the glass. When I came out, he said that he was the manager of the store across the street, and he asked me to paint the lips of his mannequins. I told him I charged 20 cents per lip, and he said, "OK!" After a few days, I had painted not only the lips of every mannequin in every store, I had also bought different brushes and many colored paints for eyebrows, cheeks, etc.

I soon had enough money to pay the hotel and my bus fare back to Dallas, where I decided to cash the return plane ticket for a bus ticket in order to see a little bit more of the United States. As the bus headed north, it got colder, and I was forced to buy a sweater and other clothing to keep warm. It was snowing in New York when I arrived. Like Gene Kelly in "Singing In The Rain," I was practically singing and dancing in the snow. What a sight!

Dr. C. Ralph Campo
Yucca, Arizona

Baby Given a Permanent Resting Place

Although Canada is an adjoining country to America, people who lived there in the 1800s were, as a rule, British subjects.

In 1861, when my Grandmother Catherine was 16, she made a trip to Iowa to visit her aunt. She planned to visit for about a month.

She liked northeast Iowa and dreaded thinking about going back to Quebec, where she and her sisters had to do the farming. Her father had died and her young brother was forced to serve in the military. One of her sisters, Winnifred, was slowly losing her sight.

Her visit was a happy one. She enjoyed the Iowa neighbors and at a house party, she met 22-year-old Jerremiah. He had come from the state of New York, where his family were woolen mills people. Iowa was strange to him, but he had relatives in the area, and of course, there was Catherine.

It seemed that the age-old adage, "love at first sight" had taken place. A whirlwind courtship ensued and they planned to be wed at the little country church known as Paint Rock.

Catherine's aunt and uncle were delighted that she could stay, and they told them of a 100-acre farm on which they could lay claim. However, there were no buildings on this fine and fertile land.

The aunt and uncle again claimed that this was a great venture, so the deal grew. They endowed them with a small start, giving them a wagon—which could be converted into living quarters—a team of horses, two milk cows, 12 laying hens, a walking plow, a bed, a homemade dresser, hay to feed the horses, feed for the hens and a harness for the team of horses.

Of course, it was to be remembered that Jerremiah was a city boy who had never been near a horse, much less harnessed one. That was where Catherine came to the rescue. She taught him how to farm. He loved it, and neither of them ever returned to their native homes. There was wood to be cut to keep them warm, and lots of rabbits and squirrels provided them with meat.

When spring came, their little farm was tilled and planted. They cut logs to begin building a house. Now they could keep nice and warm and really begin living comfortably. That log cabin was later sided and expanded. The log house became the kitchen of the house where I was born.

The summer brought fruit from the woods. Walnuts, hickory and butter nuts were abundant. Every day was a new experience. When the grain was harvested, it had to be stored until the Mississippi froze over because the only place to get wheat ground into flour was in Prairie du Chien. There were no bridges to cross.

Grandma made candles from tallow, and she often told of putting them in the windows to keep the wolves away while Grandpa was getting the wheat ground into flour. The wolves' bloodcurdling howls made a fearful sound.

Grandma was three-fourths French and one-fourth Irish. She could speak some French, but since she wanted to become an American citizen, she completely embraced English.

Their family grew to six: five boys and one girl. The youngest in the family was my father. He spent most of his life on that farm until he died at 51.

When their family had grown with the births of three little ones, Jerremiah told Catherine that they had some Indian neighbors. This tribe were en route across the state when bad weather threatened them, so they set up tepees in which to live. One of the braves had been hiding in the woods, but he was not a threat—probably more curious than anything.

One morning, there was a rap on the door. When Catherine opened it, there stood an Indian. He couldn't speak English, but he used gestures to let her know that they had a baby who was ill. It never occurred to her to refuse; she gathered up whatever home remedies she had and followed him.

They trudged through the woods to their tepee. She was dismayed when she saw a 3-month-old baby burning up with fever. She heated water in which to bathe her but her condition got worse. She made a cross and pointed heaven-ward and the mother nodded, so she baptized the baby—calling her Catherine. In less than an hour the baby died in her mother's arms. The Indians had a meeting and wondered where to bury baby Catherine. Grandma motioned to her farm and imitated someone digging a grave. They nodded because they knew they would be moving on before long.

The mother wrapped a piece of robe around the baby, but Grandma shook her head and indicated that she would be back. She went home and got one of her baby's baptismal gowns and returned to dress the little child. They carried her to our farm and dug a small grave. She was laid to rest.

Grandma made a cross to put on the grave and surrounded it with smooth rocks, which she painted with whitewash. This she did regularly. Several weeks later the Indians were gone, but at least baby Catherine had a permanent resting place. For years, until our farm was sold, we put a whitewash coat on the rocks.

When Jerremiah was 65 he died suddenly, but Catherine's love for him lived on. The night she died at age 83, she called his name and smiled.

The changes that this young couple coped with—coming to a new area—certainly tried their marriage, but it was a happy life.

Madonna Storla
Postville, Iowa

Native Americans Paid a Price

The Native American part of me knows that the immigration to the "Land of Opportunity" was a disaster for my Cherokee ancestors.

My great-great-grandmother was uprooted with her family. While it was unfortunate for the larger part of the family, it benefitted her in another way. She was young, and married into my paternal ancestors' family. I wonder what she'd think of my sister, Morning Sun; my brother, Hunts The Deer; and me, Night Star. Would she be happy that I am now part of the TSALAGIYI NVDAGI, the Texas Cherokee?

I think she'd be glad that I, too, have a happy married life with someone whose family also came to the Land of Opportunity. But let's never forget the price Native Americans paid so that everyone could come to this country.

Jo Ann Miller
Huffman, Texas

MY FOLKS AND THE LAND OF OPPORTUNITY

INDEX